the busy mom's guide to
spiritual survival

D0834670

the busy mom's guide to
spiritual survival

Kelli B. Trujillo

wesleyan
publishing
house

Indianapolis, Indiana

Copyright © 2007 by Wesleyan Publishing House
Published by Wesleyan Publishing House
Indianapolis, Indiana 46250
Printed in the United States of America

ISBN-13: 978-0-89827-346-5
ISBN-10: 0-89827-346-3

Library of Congress Cataloging-in-Publication Data

Trujillo, Kelli B.
  The busy mom's guide to spiritual survival / Kelli B. Trujillo.
     p. cm.
  ISBN-13: 978-0-89827-346-5
  ISBN-10: 0-89827-346-3
  1. Mothers--Religious life. 2. Motherhood--Religious
aspects--Christianity. I. Title.

BV4529.18.T78 2007
248.8'45--dc22

2006100235

For my sister, Kara, as she begins
the adventure of motherhood

contents

acknowledgments

This book would not have been possible without the help, encouragement, and inspiration of many people.

Thank you to my many friends who've struggled alongside me, striving to live their lives as Jesus followers and super moms. I'm especially grateful to Julie Algate, Emily Cetola, Jennifer Derksen, Katie Greiwe, Rachel Hibbard, Amie Hollmann, Susan Nathan, Christin Nevins, Carolyn Rosenau, Amy Simpson, Becky Smith, and Stacy Weikal, who shared their candid thoughts and honest stories with me as this book was in the germination stage.

Thank you, also, to my writer friends Joy-Elizabeth Lawrence and Kate Holburn for reviewing the first draft of my manuscript and providing creative, thought-provoking feedback.

I couldn't have spent time working away at the laptop without the help of the world's best (free!) babysitters: my parents, Bob and Jeanne Blahnik; and my parents-in-law, David and Anita Trujillo.

Thank you to my two beautiful children, Davis and Lucia, for the joy they've brought to my life.

Thank you to my editor, Larry Wilson, my publisher, Don Cady, and the rest of the awesome team at Wesleyan Publishing House for believing in this idea, for fine-tuning my manuscript, and especially for caring about and investing in the spiritual formation of busy moms.

And most important, thank you to my husband and best friend, David Trujillo, for your fabulous partnership in this adventure called parenting; for your tireless encouragement, support, and theological insights during the writing process; and for journeying by my side along the narrow road.

introduction

motherhood:
a faith wasteland?

As I prepared for the birth of my first child, I decided to ready myself for the harrowing experience by interviewing some friends who'd already given birth. I asked all the usual questions: What happened when? How did it feel? Were you scared? What were the best and worst parts?

One of my friends, Melanie, had had two children and had given birth au naturel both times. *She is definitely an expert*, I thought and soaked up her advice like a dry sponge. She candidly told me about her experiences, infusing her stories with spiritual insight. She talked about Jesus and the pain he endured to give us new life—how as mothers we, too, go through extreme pain to bring a child into the world. She told me about the Bible verses she had memorized and repeated over and over during labor. She spoke of the sheer delight of holding her newborn kids and about the immense responsibility of raising a child in the nurture and admonition of the Lord. My eyes glassed over, my heart sang, and I felt certain that giving birth would be the most profound spiritual experience of my life.

Then reality hit.

I'll spare you the gory details, but I will say that no Bible verse ever graced my lips during the actual delivery process. Giving birth was definitely not the spiritual high that I had imagined. Yet my friend was right on one account: Holding my newborn child for the first time was a truly profound—and overwhelming—spiritual experience. *This child is mine?* I thought. *Oh God . . . help!* Immediately diapers, nursing, diapers, burping, diapers, sleepless nights, and more diapers took over my life. In an instant, everything had changed. Gone were the lengthy morning study times, the reading, journaling, and note taking. (Who can concentrate after only four hours' sleep?) Gone were the penetrating conversations with Christian friends. (Who can listen prayerfully with a child dumping cereal on the floor?) Gone were the moments of deep personal reflection when my soul was consumed with the search for God. Now my identity was swallowed up in caring for the little person who had taken center stage in our family's life.

My spiritual journey had run smack-dab into a brick wall called motherhood. Sometimes it seemed to have completely stopped. I felt as if the tiniest crumb—a thirty-second prayer here, a short Bible verse there, a Sunday morning sermon (heard with one ear— the other tuned to the church nursery) was all the spiritual nourishment I would get for the next eighteen years. I soon came to a realization shared by many Christian mothers of young children: Although motherhood is a deeply profound spiritual experience, it can also become a faith wasteland.

But it doesn't have to be!

God created parenting to be an immense responsibility, but I don't believe he intended to press the spiritual pause button on a new mother's heart. Our spiritual formation shouldn't be on hold until our children enter kindergarten—or go off to college. Motherhood should *renovate* our spiritual lives, not demolish them. When you become a mother, you are still *you*. Your soul still thirsts for God, your heart still yearns to sing his praises, your unique identity and gifts do not suddenly become obsolete or focused solely on your child. You're still meant to press on, to run the race, to take hold of the prize. (See 2 Timothy 4:7 and Philippians 3:12–14.) Christ is still in you, the "hope of glory" (Col. 1:27)! Your spiritual journey doesn't end when your child's journey begins.

To *renovate*, by definition, is to make fresh or sound again, as though new; to clean up, and replace worn or broken parts; to repair, refresh, revive.[1] From the rich teaching of Scripture and from the time-tested practices of the Church, we discover the basic habits and foundational practices essential for spiritual growth. These habits— the spiritual disciplines—serve as catalysts in the renovation process. Some of these classic disciplines, such as service, are inherent in motherhood. Others, such as Bible study, meditation, and solitude (you've got to be kidding!) seem incompatible with a life so jam-packed with activities and the demands of care giving that you can't always find time to change out of your own pj's.

Instead of ignoring these seemingly impractical disciplines and surviving on a subsistence diet of spiritual crumbs, let's give these spiritual practices a just-for-moms makeover. So go ahead: Scrap the mental picture of a hermit living in a desert cave, a nun cloistered in an abbey, or a pastor quietly passing the hours in a study. Instead, take a look at your everyday reality as a working mom or a stay-at-home mom and begin to see your joyful, tiring, and busy life as fertile ground for amazing spiritual growth. Impossible? Don't you believe it!

Let's take a fresh look at some classic spiritual disciplines through the eyes of the busiest person on earth, a mother of small children. We'll find out why these practices are so important for maintaining a vibrant spiritual life, we'll examine biblical examples of each one, and we'll discover some realistic, doable ways to implement these disciplines in everyday life—with kids. As a bonus, we'll also garner some age-appropriate ideas for fostering the natural growth of spiritual disciplines in the lives of our children.

Here's one suggestion before we get started. Undertake this journey of discovery in the company of at least one other mom. All Christians need fellowship, and that is especially true for mothers with young children. While this book will be a great benefit even if studied alone, it will be even more valuable as the starting point for a discussion of spiritual growth among you and your Christian friends. At the end of each chapter, you'll find ten easy-to-try ideas to pick from, as well as discussion questions you can use to talk with other moms about the ideas in this book.

As you incorporate spiritual disciplines into your daily rhythm, you'll experience the beginnings of spiritual renovation. The Holy Spirit will replace worn or broken spiritual parts. Your deepening relationship with God will refresh and revive you. You'll offer a rich and vibrant spiritual example to your children. And you'll cherish God's faithful presence with you through each moment of motherhood.

So hop on board—let's start the journey!

1

discipline that has nothing to do with spanking

"The threes can be much more terrible than the twos."

This week I realized that my son's pediatrician was right! Just days after my son, Davis's, third birthday, it appeared that his mind had somehow been wiped clean of the basic human skills I'd labored so hard to teach him over the past year: listening, obeying, using words to express feelings. Now every other word out of his mouth was either *no* or *why*. But what I heard most often was the sound of toys ricocheting off the walls as he threw them around his room. The last straw was the surprise body slam I received after picking out the wrong pair of socks for him to wear. After the five-hundredth instance of sitting him on the naughty chair and listening to him wail in frustration, I was so discouraged with being a mother that I nearly joined him in a good time-out cry. *Why isn't my parenting working?* I wondered. *Is it worth it to go through all the hard work of disciplining him? Am I a failure?*

Have you ever been there?

Nobody likes discipline. Kids don't like receiving it, and moms don't like dishing it out. It may be necessary, but none of us enjoys disciplining her children. After a long day of playing "bad cop," we usually end up feeling discouraged, downhearted, and emotionally exhausted. This is not the joy of motherhood we'd always envisioned.

Interestingly, we often feel the same way when we reflect on our spiritual lives and the inevitable contrast between our desire to grow and the time-crunched reality of daily life. Check out what these moms had to say to see if you can relate.

Graduate Student and Working Mother of Two: When I stop to think about it, I realize that I just don't spend enough time or energy devoting myself to prayer, Bible study, and other spiritual disciplines. That drives me to feel guilty, spiritually dry, and frustrated.

Wife and Stay-at-Home Mom of a Newborn: It has been difficult at times to be spiritually plugged in. As the wife of a pastor, my lack of spiritual discipline makes me feel hypocritical. So many people are trying to tell me who I'm supposed to be and what my role should be.

Stay-at-Home Mother of Two-Year-Old Twins: I feel like God shouldn't have to listen to my prayers and concerns if I rarely make time for him or for reading the Bible. Emotionally, it's draining because I pile on the guilt and then avoid making changes because I fear that since I can't stick with something, it's just going to lead to more guilt.

Working Mother of Two, in Christian Ministry: Not practicing regular spiritual growth habits led to a very dry and dark time, my feeling depressed, unable to pull things together, and distant from people. I felt inferior to others spiritually. This inferiority feeling was especially difficult because I am in Christian ministry.

Did you hear that? Guilty. Frustrated. Hypocritical. Drained. Depressed. Spiritually inferior. That's exactly how I felt when I began reading a classic book on spiritual disciplines while my first child was an infant. I was excited at first and so ready to deepen my spiritual life; yet as I turned each page, I felt worse and worse and worse. *I can't do any of this*, I realized. *I don't have the time.* Almost immediately I began to question my own spiritual integrity. *Am I just making excuses? Am I a hypocrite? Am I putting on a spiritual show for others when in reality my spiritual life is a joke?* I tried to press on with the book, but the discouragement became overwhelming. I closed the book, put it on the shelf, and settled down with the sad conclusion that spiritual disciplines just weren't for me. In effect, I placed myself on a spiritual naughty chair— wallowing in self-inflicted feelings of guilt and failure. That's not exactly what I had in mind when I picked up a book on spiritual "discipline." I was looking for a book that would help me know God better, not one that would make me feel hopeless about the state of my spiritual life.

If you understand that feeling, then this book is most definitely for you. If you're a spiritual June Cleaver with your home and faith perfectly under control, you can put this book away. But if you've dreamed of growing deeper yet have felt held back by the realities of your life, then, please, keep reading. But first, you've got to agree to Rule 1. Ready?

Rule 1: No self-pity, self-induced guilt, or feelings of inadequacy allowed!

That means None. Zip. Zilch. Zero. Nada. This is not a start-reading, feel-guilty, give-up, close-book kind of book. This is a book about real life, real struggles, and the real needs we all have. So get up off that naughty chair and get ready for a spiritual booster shot.

15

why we do this

In a basic sense, there is some connection between the type of discipline you give your children and the spiritual disciplines: Both are actions that result in growth toward maturity. Yet beyond that similarity, the spiritual disciplines we're talking about here are completely different from discipline that has the negative connotation of punishment or chastisement. Although we use the same English word for both types of discipline, the Bible uses several Greek words to communicate more specific connotations. For example, Hebrews 12:6–7 states, "'the Lord disciplines those he loves, and he punishes everyone he accepts as a son.' Endure hardship as discipline; God is treating you as sons. For what son is not disciplined by his father?" Here the writer uses the Greek words *paideuo* and *paideia*, which can also be translated as "chastise," "instruct," or "correct."

But as we practice the spiritual disciplines, we're aiming for a different concept of discipline, one communicated by the Greek terms *gumnazo* and *askeo*, which are used in Scripture. Gumnazo—from which we derive the English word *gymnasium*—means discipline in the sense of athletic exercise and training. So we're talking about spiritual sweat here: regular "workouts" that keep our faith in shape. This is the word Paul used when he urged Timothy, "*train* yourself to be godly. For physical training is of some value, but godliness has value for all things, holding promise for both the present life and the life to come" (1 Tim. 4:7–8, emphasis added). This is the connotation the writer of Hebrews intended when he prodded his readers, saying, "Anyone who lives on milk, being still an infant, is not acquainted with the teaching about righteousness. But solid food is for the mature, who by constant use have *trained* themselves to distinguish good from evil" (Heb. 5:13–14, emphasis added).

Askeo indicates the discipline of a master craftsman who employs skill, persistent determination, and great effort to turn raw material into a piece of art. Imagine here a sword smith laboring late into the night over a bed of white-hot coals in order to turn a chunk of raw steel into a perfectly shaped weapon. This is exercise, training, and discipline completed at great effort and personal cost. This is the concept behind Paul's statement in Acts 24:16: "So I *strive* always to keep my conscience clear before God and man" (emphasis added).

Discipline is never undertaken for its own sake. We don't discipline children just for kicks; and when we exercise to lose those too-familiar pregnancy pounds, we know our training and sweat are for a good purpose. It's the same with spiritual disciplines. There are some good reasons to push ourselves spiritually.

to know god

The primary reason for practicing spiritual disciplines is simple: to draw close to God; to experience deep connection and intimate companionship with the Father, the Son, and the Holy Spirit. Jesus said, "Abide in me, and I in you. As the branch cannot bear fruit by itself, unless it abides in the vine, neither can you, unless you abide in me" (John 15:4 ESV). By integrating spiritual disciplines into our lives, we're able to *abide* in Christ—to connect to the nourishment of the Vine.

to grow like jesus

We practice the disciplines also as acts of discipleship. We train ourselves by doing what Jesus taught when he said, "If you keep my commandments, you will abide in my love, just as I have kept my Father's commandments and abide in his love" (John 15:10 ESV). The spiritual disciplines are drawn from Jesus' commands and teachings as well as from his personal example. As his disciples, we learn from the very practices central to Jesus' life and we imitate them. We train ourselves to become like our teacher, Jesus. "A student is not above his teacher, but everyone who is fully trained will be like his teacher" (Luke 6:40).

to be transformed

Another reason we practice spiritual disciplines is that they are the means through which the Holy Spirit changes us. As we grow from spiritual babes toward spiritual maturity, our lives are transformed; and the disciplines are one means God uses to "grow us up" in faith, holiness, and Christlikeness.

to be examples

As mothers, we practice the disciplines in order to be examples for our children. As we live out the spiritual disciplines we can say to our children, "Follow my example, as I follow the example of Christ" (1 Cor. 11:1).

avoiding wrong motivation

Exercise and a regimen of healthy eating will help you improve your physical health, but if your aim is to change your eye color, height, or tone deafness, then you'll certainly end up disappointed. When we exercise physically, we must have the proper goals in mind; we need to be realistic and honest about what our efforts can accomplish. Similarly, if you have the wrong aims in mind when you practice these disciplines, you're sure to feel let down when those intended "results" don't materialize.

reward

Our goal in practicing the spiritual disciplines is not to merit God's favor or earn God's grace. These aren't chores we do in order to win stickers or earn an allowance of spiritual benefits. We are saved through faith and not by works that we do (Eph. 2:8–9). God loves us because it is God's nature to love, not because we have bettered ourselves to the point of being pleasing in his sight. His grace is a gift we receive through faith in the sufficient work of Christ on the cross.

19

punishment

Furthermore, our goal in practicing spiritual disciplines is not to punish ourselves for sin. Self-deprivation, no matter how consistently practiced or how extreme, cannot erase sin. Jesus took the punishment for our sin upon himself when he died on the cross. He accomplished the ultimate act of forgiveness. We need not punish ourselves in order to rid ourselves of sin or our sinful cravings.

achievement

Spiritual disciplines are not a way to become holy or righteous by our own efforts. It is true that they are an avenue for life transformation, but it is not we who make the changes—it is God's Spirit within us who changes us. As we do the work of exercising faith, God does his work in us.

pleasure

It feels good to grow spiritually, but we don't practice the disciplines in order to experience the good feelings that can result from them. Practicing the disciplines can lead to feelings of contentment, peace, and closeness with God, but these are mere byproducts. For there will also be times when the disciplines work quietly, not seeming to do much for you. Sometimes you'll feel the same as you did before, or even worse. So if your focus is on feelings, prepare to be disappointed.

escape

No matter how appealing it may sound to get away for a few moments of silence or solitude, we don't practice the spiritual disciplines as a means of escaping the hectic circumstances of our lives. This is not your ticket to a retreat into an imaginary, monk-like cell of spiritual bliss. The disciplines are a part of your real life—for your nitty-gritty, spit-up cleaning, finger-painting, lullaby-singing life.

the disciplines

Depending on your church background, you've likely been presented at some point with a de facto list of spiritual disciplines—the practices that are considered essential for spiritual growth in your tradition. Some churches emphasize prayer and Bible study as the keys to spiritual growth; others stress the experiences of worship and fellowship; yet others key on the acts of financial giving and serving others as the identifying marks of a true Christian. Overbusy and highly stressed as we usually are, we moms tend to latch on to the basic practices emphasized in our church tradition to the neglect of other practices presented in Scripture. When our repetitive diet of these few spiritual "nutrients" leaves us spiritually weak, we're naturally led to question ourselves and surrender to feelings of despair and discouragement.

A basic survey of both the practices of God's people in the Old Testament and the teachings of Jesus and the apostles in the New Testament presents us with a much broader and more integrated perspective on discipleship. We discover communal feasts and celebrations, regular periods of fasting, compelling acts of giving and service, lives of radical solitude and simplicity, convicting examples of hospitality, and more. In this book we'll explore fifteen of the disciplines practiced by Christians in Scripture and throughout Church history.

- Silence
- Solitude
- Scriptural Learning
- Prayer
- Meditation
- Life Change
- Evangelism
- Hospitality

- Service
- Simplicity
- Stewardship
- Fasting
- Fellowship
- Worship
- Celebration

21

There are other disciplines, but I've narrowed our focus to these fifteen central ones. That's not because the others are unimportant but because I believe these fifteen are foundational to our spiritual growth as women and mothers and, believe it or not, because they're all compatible in some way, shape, or form with life as a busy mom of young kids.

By the way, now would be a good time to introduce Rule 2. Ready?

Rule 2: No overachieving allowed!

Your goal in reading this book is not to incorporate all the spiritual disciplines into your life at one time. Any effort along these lines will leave you feeling more stressed and will make your family think you've been brainwashed at some wacky spiritual self-improvement seminar. Furthermore, you won't succeed. You'll only make yourself feel guilty and inadequate—which takes us back to Rule 1.

Think of this book as a spiritual disciplines buffet; as you read and consider each chapter, it will be as if you're visiting a buffet table and sampling a tidbit of every entrée before you. Some of the tastes will be totally new to you and could take some getting used to; others will be old favorites—comfort foods that warm your heart and put a smile on your face. So as you read, commit yourself to trying each discipline in some way so that you'll get a taste of what all are like. And give yourself a realistic goal (in accordance with Rule 2), like focusing on just one discipline each week (or each month), implementing only one or two Try It ideas at a time, or meeting twice a month with a small group of other moms to discuss one discipline. By the time you've completed the book, you will have tasted and gained initial familiarity with a bounty of spiritual practices.

Then, as with all good buffets, you can go back to the table for a second helping and zero in on the disciplines God is leading you toward. Sometimes God may draw you to focus on an area of spiritual weakness so that the exercise of a specific discipline will strengthen feeble spiritual muscles. For example, if you're tempted by materialism and consumerism, the Holy Spirit might prompt you to focus on the disciplines of simplicity and fasting. Or if you've had a week that's incredibly chaotic, God may prompt you to get refocused by implementing the disciplines of silence and solitude.

At other times God may lead you to find nourishment in disciplines that match your spiritual strengths, passions, and desires. You may feel drawn to expand on your already consistent experiences of worship, to deepen the level of fellowship in an existing close Christian friendship, or to incorporate more regular times of meditation on Scripture into your regular prayer habits.

The good news is that this is one buffet table where you *should* keep on going back to fill your plate. This training and striving through spiritual disciplines is the spiritual "solid food . . . for the mature, who *by constant use* have trained themselves" (Heb. 5:14, emphasis added). For us moms, that "constant use" likely won't be hours spent in practicing the disciplines each day; we simply don't have that much time. But you *can* commit yourself to implementing disciplines at a pace that fits your busy life. Out of the raw material of your life—the sweet, everyday chaos of motherhood—you *can* strive (askeo) to imitate Christ and abide intimately with him. Through the Holy Spirit's work in you, your life can be renovated into a work of art before God.

talk about it

Discuss these questions with a friend or a small group of other moms.

1. In what way has being a mom had a positive impact on your spiritual life?

2. Has your role as a mom had a negative impact on your life? If so, how?

3. Can you relate to the feelings of the four moms quoted in this chapter? What effect does guilt or other negative feelings have on your own efforts toward spiritual growth?

4. Does the word *discipline* have a negative or positive connotation in your mind? Why?

5. What are you most excited about as you start your process of spiritual renovation? Why?

try it

In each of the upcoming chapters, you'll find ten Try It ideas to choose from to help you implement each discipline. As a way of getting started, take some time to fill out this personal evaluation.

1. Below is a list of spiritual disciplines, Christian practices, and spiritual growth habits. Mark each of these practices to indicate if they are a *frequent* part of your life as a mother, something you're *occasionally* able to do, something you're *rarely* able to incorporate into your real life, or something you're *never* able to do or have never done before.

spiritual discipline	frequently	occasionally	rarely	never
intentional times of silence				
intentional times of solitude				
scriptural learning (such as Bible study or Scripture memorization)				
prayer				
christian meditation or contemplation				
self-evaluation and life application				
service				
evangelism				
hospitality				
simplicity (choosing to live simply)				
stewardship and giving				
fasting				
fellowship				
worship				
celebration				

2. Of those you marked *Frequently* or *Occasionally*, which has been most helpful for your spiritual growth? How has it impacted your faith?

3. Of those you marked *Rarely* or *Never*, which disciplines do you most wish you were able to incorporate into your life?

4. As you reflect on the current state of your spiritual life, in what areas do you most want to grow? How do you think spiritual disciplines might help you do that?

5. Consider sharing your self-evaluation with a friend or small group.

25

2

silence and solitude

Aahhh . . . it was finally *quiet*. Things felt still. At last I could breathe. After a crazy weekend of hosting houseguests, teaching Sunday school, cramming to meet a writing deadline, cooking, cleaning, and mothering, here I was in my moment of bliss, seated beneath a luxurious maple tree in the city park. As that long-lost sense of relaxation washed over me, I smiled at my young son, who was beside me in his stroller, and relished the opportunity to slow down, to breathe deep, and to just be with God.

The sun shone brightly and a fall breeze shuffled the colorful leaves at my feet. Yet as that gentle breeze reached my nose, I sensed that something wasn't right. I sniffed again, then followed the foul odor—toward my son. He grimaced. The distinctly unpleasant smell belonged to him.

"I can't believe this," I muttered, rolling my eyes in disgust. "My one peaceful moment is ruined by a dirty diaper." I reached for the diaper bag at my side. It wasn't there. I looked beneath the stroller; it wasn't there either. In my hurry to pack up and head for a moment of sanity at the park, I forgot the mother's essential survival kit. I had violated the most basic tenet of early motherhood: I was alone in the woods—without wet wipes!

Within seconds my son's grimace turned to a whine and then a full-blown howl. My moment of silence now kaput, I gingerly loaded him into the minivan, chuckling at my own carelessness. And as I drove toward home, determined to laugh instead of cry, I wondered, *Will I ever have peace and quiet in my life?*

Every mother of young children can relate to that feeling. Between caring for kids, managing the house, and tackling work or other responsibilities, the idyllic quietness of heart and deep communion with God we long for can seem like a mirage, a perpetually unattainable goal. Real life with real kids is seldom quiet, and dedicated moms are hardly ever alone. For us, even using the bathroom can become a family affair! Of all the classic spiritual disciplines, silence and solitude can seem the most unrealistic for a mother with young children.

In many ways these disciplines are incongruous with parenthood. It's not possible to live as a hermit and bond with your children. It's not possible to take a vow of silence and simultaneously supply your children with the verbal affirmation, songs, and bedtime stories they need. As one friend put it, "Solitude and silence are the least compatible disciplines with my life as a mom. Yet I long to be able to spend time alone in quietness; I have a really hard time listening to God without it." We all face this reality—when our lives are filled with noise, we feel that we are never alone with God. It certainly is hard to sense God's presence and listen to God's voice with children crying in the background.

> The person who wants to arrive at interiority and spirituality has to leave the crowd behind and spend some time with Jesus.
>
> —Thomas à Kempis

Yet these very disciplines—silence and solitude—are the essential starting place for deepening our spiritual growth, for they help us create a way of life that is conducive to real communion with God. Author Dallas Willard named quiet solitude as the bedrock discipline on which the others are built when he wrote,

> Solitude is generally the most fundamental at the beginning of the spiritual life, and it must be returned to again and again as that life develops. . . . Just try fasting, prayer, service, giving, or even celebration without the preparation accomplished in withdrawal, and you will soon be thrown into despair by your efforts, very likely abandoning your attempt altogether.[1]

So is it pointless to read this book? Given the fact you can never get alone and practice solitude, there's no way to succeed at the other disciplines, right? *Wrong!* There are ways for real-life moms to practice the disciplines of silence and solitude—we just need to give them a mom-friendly makeover.

silence and solitude redefined

What does silence mean in the life of a mom? We can find an answer by examining the powerful example of a biblical woman, Mary of Bethany. Although it appears that Mary did not have children, she was responsible for managing a family home. Our glimpse into her life in Luke 10:38–42 will show much about coping with the many demands and stresses mothers face. Mary and her sister, Martha, had a very special dinner guest: Jesus! In order to prepare a meal for him, they had to attend to a number of important matters. Remember that back then they didn't have refrigerators or microwaves. Preparing for a houseguest was a lot more work. Yet to her sister's chagrin, Mary chose to turn away from the hustle and bustle of preparation and sit quietly to listen to Jesus, content and present before him. And Jesus commended her for it, saying, "Only one thing is needed. Mary has chosen what is better, and it will not be taken away from her" (verse 42). Can we, like Mary, choose the better way of living?

The core of the discipline of silence is quietness of heart. It is choosing to be still at the Lord's feet, as Mary did. Picture your heart as a lake. How does the surface appear to you? Is the water in constant motion, with choppy waves sloshing about as the winds of circumstance whip the water first this way and then that? Or is the water calm, still, and quiet? It is the calm lake that brilliantly reflects a sunrise like a mirror. Similarly, a heart that is still before God reflects his glory. Silence is choosing to be still before God.

29

Depending on the ages of your children, times of solitude may already be a natural part of your day when your kids take naps or go to school. But solitude as a spiritual discipline is more than being physically alone. Solitude, like silence, is a matter of the heart. It is a purposeful withdrawal from the company of others in which we recognize that we are not truly alone but are in the presence of Almighty God.

As you set about practicing silence and solitude, you'll probably experience an initial discomfort with being alone. You'll start to recognize that you have become dependent on your children, friends, television, radio, or other social interactions to occupy your mind. You may use these things as a shield to keep tough questions or challenging issues from invading your thoughts. Yet as you endure that initial discomfort, your persistent efforts to practice silence and solitude will till the soil of your heart, readying it for transformation. Habitual times of silence and solitude will lead you to

Heightened God Awareness. You'll understand that God is present and that this time isn't meaningless or empty.

Deeper Self-Awareness. You'll develop a sense that "this is me." You'll face yourself and see glaring areas where you fall short of God's best or feel convicted of sin. At other times you'll experience delight and joy in the you God created.

Spiritual Refreshment. As a result of solitude and silence, you'll feel re-energized and more deeply connected to God.

Contentment. As your mind and heart become centered on God, you'll sift out the chaff of daily worries and consuming to-do lists, allowing yourself to just be.

30

Refocused Priorities. As you are silent in God's presence, you'll start to realize what is truly important and, therefore, worth your effort and time.

Communication with the Holy Spirit. When a person is busy, always with others, and continually surrounded by the noise of daily life, it is extremely difficult to listen to God's voice. In silence and solitude God's still small voice can be heard (1 Kings 19:12).

kids need it too

In this fast-paced and harried world, a little silence and solitude are also just what the pediatrician ordered. Silence and solitude are important not only for *your* spiritual growth but also are critical for your children's social, mental, emotional, and spiritual development.

Solitude for a young child can be something as simple as intentionally spending time alone with a coloring book. Or it could be a more structured time of rest during the day in which the child either naps or lies quietly in bed. Silence can be a break from the sensory stimulation of television, CDs, or noisy toys to instead sing soothing songs or just snuggle together. It could also mean fostering quietness in a child's heart by talking about fears or worries and praying with Mom or Dad.

The silence of a quieted heart is a key element in the development of a child's personality and ability to exercise self-control. A child's capacity to be calm and emotionally still can be a great help when he or she deals with cranky moods that are often caused by being over-tired or overstimulated. Health researchers at Duke University have concluded that many children live overprogrammed, stress-filled lives and that this stress contributes directly to behavior problems and even physical illness. The Duke researchers recommend that parents provide children with a regular time to participate in quiet, calm activities—time when parents "give [their] children time to just *be*."[2] From a Christian perspective, the goal is not for kids simply to be alone or to be quiet; it is to regularly have times of being calm physically, emotionally, and spiritually in order to center on God.

putting it into action: mom-friendly ideas

The good news is that there are doable ways both to weave the threads of silence and solitude into the tapestry of daily life and to introduce these values to your children. Here are a few ideas—some are simple and some are more challenging. All require focus, effort, and persistence.

refocus "wasted" time

When I worked outside the home, I had even less time for silence or solitude than I do now as a work-from-home mom. Between the demands of coworkers, looming project deadlines, and my own desire to pack in lots of quality family time from the moment I stepped in the door at night, setting aside time to be quiet and alone was forced to the bottom of the priority list.

Then one day while driving to work, I had a "duh" moment. It dawned on me that my twenty-minute commute was a daily opportunity for some God-time that I was totally missing! I was alone—no husband, no baby, no coworkers—so it was a golden opportunity to quiet my heart. I began the habit of turning off the radio and driving in silence. Sometimes I talked aloud to God. Sometimes I sang songs. Often I was just quiet. In that capsule of time, wedged between the two worlds I was juggling—home and work—I could leave both aside and just be. Granted, the time was short. Bad traffic often threw a wrench into my plan. And coffee was definitely a requirement. Yet on many mornings, I walked into work feeling focused and tuned-in to the Holy Spirit's voice.

A morning commute is one opportunity to refocus what seems like wasted time on the spiritual disciplines of silence and solitude; there are others. As unspiritual as it may sound, your morning or evening shower is another opportunity for spiritual growth. If you are a mom with small children, this is one of the only times you'll find yourself completely alone. Even if you have only five minutes, you can turn those minutes over to God. Instead of checking through a mental to-do list or spacing out, focus your energy on quieting your heart and mind. Remind yourself of God's presence, of his awesome power, of his amazing love. Put a Bible verse, such as Psalm 37:7, in a ziplock bag and affix it to the showerhead with a string. Read this hope-on-a-rope as you begin your time of quietness. As you finish your shower, ask God to help you maintain quietness of heart throughout the day, no matter what events or frustrations threaten to whip up a heart storm.

In which moments in your weekly routine do you find yourself alone? During your workout? while mowing the lawn? doing laundry? weeding the garden? You can establish the habit of communing with God through silence and solitude simply by repurposing those windows of time.

get outside

Spending time outdoors provides an excellent opportunity to heighten your God-awareness level and quiet a fretting, preoccupied heart. If you are in the habit of walking for exercise, consider your walks a time in God's presence. Be alert and observe the world around you—notice cloud formations, a cool breeze, or neighborhood flowers. Let concerns go from your mind.

You can also use God-focused time outdoors as a powerful way to introduce your children to the value of silence and solitude. When you take your kids with you on walks around the neighborhood, point out God's power in the weather; share words of affirmation and encouragement; or stop and study bugs, leaves, and dirt. Walk side-by-side without speaking, or take a break to lie down together, look at the sky, and talk about heaven or sing simple worship songs. These times together will help your children develop an awareness of God's presence all around them. Though the walks are unlikely to literally be silent, they will foster quietness of heart.

33

get away from it all

Spending focused, intentional times away from others is one of the primary ways you can experience silence and solitude, though these times will probably be few and far between. Some friends of mine—Emily and Jennifer—have come up with a great way to "leave the crowd behind" and spend some time with Jesus. Each Tuesday morning they do a babysitting trade: one mom takes care of all the kids while the other mom has some "time off" to spend alone with God. It's relaxing, refreshing, and free! Making an arrangement like this one will not only allow you some much needed time in quietness with God but will also enrich the spiritual life of a sister in Christ. As one friend reminds us, "We're all in this together!"

Christin, who is a part-time working mom, gets away for moments of silence and solitude by taking an annual vacation with her husband, Adam—without their kids! During their trip, they agree that they will each read the same Christian book. They spend some time each day away from each other to read, pray, think, be quiet, and connect with God. Then they come together to share their experiences, discuss the book, and grow closer to God as a couple. Though these escapes from life with the kids come only about once a year, Christin has found the experiences to be so meaningful and refreshing that they sustain her for a long time when she returns to "real life."

You, too, can arrange some focused, intentional time with God. See if your husband is willing to plan a spiritually focused vacation, even if it's just overnight. In the meantime, try to schedule a time when someone can watch your kids so you can be alone with God. Set aside a one- to three-hour block of time for a personal adventure in silence. If you'd like, take along a journal, Bible, or hymnbook, then go to a park or other place where you can be alone and untroubled by life's hustle and bustle. Sit, rest, be with God. It will seem boring at times, but push through it. Try to keep your heart in an attitude of contentment, stilled before God (Ps. 37:7).

take advantage of nap times

I was speaking to my friend Katie on the phone about some serious subjects—kids, God, and good books. The speed with which we covered each topic would've stunned some observers. What's the hurry? Mothers, however, would have realized our motivation: We were cramming our social life into the fifteen-minute window during which our children's naps overlapped. A child's naptime is a precious jewel of time when a mom can get stuff done, read a good book, talk to a friend, spend time in the Word, or just be herself.

Even when your child outgrows daily naps, which usually happens between the ages of three and five,[3] your pattern of taking a break during the day doesn't have to end. Consider replacing the nap with a brief quiet time for your child. If your child is young, use a baby monitor or a gate on the door to keep tabs on him. Set him in bed, but tell yourself it's OK if he gets out of bed to look at books or play with toys. Tell older kids they are to stay in their room until you come and get them, and set a reasonable time limit based on your child's ability to be alone—from five minutes up to one hour. Use this time to get your thoughts in order and quiet your heart before God. Then stay focused on enjoying God's presence with you as you read, study Scripture, or go about daily tasks like vacuuming or paying bills.

This much-needed break for you will also teach your child invaluable skills—the ability to entertain himself, to play creatively and use imagination, and to soothe himself—not to mention the physical and emotional benefits of rest. Often after even a short quiet time, a child's mood will be greatly improved for the remainder of the day.

limit media consumption

I admit it: I'm a TV junkie at heart. If left to my own devices, I'd watch way more television than is good for me. In most American homes, the TV is on for nearly eight hours per day.[4] Why do we watch so much TV? Often it is to avoid the discomfort that accompanies solitude. When the television is on, it's as if we have adult company. Instead of being alone in the kitchen, we're discussing books with Oprah or getting counseling from Dr. Phil. Also, relying on the television or radio seemingly helps to avoid the pitfall of boredom; we're entertained minute by minute. In reality excessive media consumption perpetuates boredom and promotes a mind-set that is contrary to spiritual growth, making us increasingly unable to entertain ourselves and progressively more uncomfortable with quietness.

Television can also be bad for young children. Because of the potentially hazardous effects of TV watching on brain development, the American Academy of Pediatrics recommends that children two and younger *never* watch television. For kids older than two, the Academy suggests a maximum of one to two hours of educational television daily.[5] However, in most American households, young children watch about four hours of TV on a given day.[6] Spiritually, excessive use of TV and other electronic media produces the same result in kids' lives as it does in adults': it stifles the imagination, increases their discomfort with quietness, hikes up their need to be visually or aurally stimulated, and often negatively affects their mood.

> It is a frightful satire and an epigram on the modern age that the only use it knows for solitude is to make it a punishment, a jail sentence.
>
> —Søren Kierkegaard

So try a family media fast. Set a specific time frame, such as one week, during which your family will consume no media whatsoever. Or try no TV on Thursdays, or maybe go one month without media entertainment. But be warned: If your children are used to watching a lot of TV, creating a media fast is sure to demand a great deal of extra effort on your part! To replace the TV time, they'll need your attention and creative activities such as reading books together, playing outside, or going to the zoo. If you fill the empty time by engaging your children, they'll soon forget they even wanted to watch TV.

Another way to cut back on the overdose of electronic media is to relocate the TV. One of the best choices our family ever made was to put the TV on a roller cart and store it in the closet. This simple change of location makes me more conscious that watching TV is a choice because it now requires an extra effort to roll it out and turn it on. That often helps me kick my dazed self-control into gear and "just say no." Though I still occasionally struggle with wanting to zone out with a favorite show, the limits I've set for myself and the bulky TV cart's location in the closet have made a world of difference in my ability to keep the TV off and spend time in more wholesome and spiritually fulfilling activities.

By limiting media consumption (or cutting it out altogether for set periods of time), both you and your children will benefit. You'll experience peace instead of discomfort when it's quiet in the house. You'll become more naturally aware of God's presence.

37

be still, my soul

Invariably, your efforts toward establishing patterns of silence and solitude will be thwarted by the stuff of parenting—sick children, fights between siblings, a barrage of "urgent" events and activities. That's OK. Your goal is not to achieve something; it is simply to be, like Mary, content at the feet of Jesus.

We all have moments when we need to remind ourselves to be still, to breathe, to rest in contentment before God. I love the words of Katharina A. von Schlegel's hymn "Be Still, My Soul," for they capture so well the internal dialogue I often have about putting forth the effort to be alone and quiet before God.

> Be still, my soul: the Lord is on thy side
> Bear patiently the cross of grief or pain.
> Leave to thy God to order and provide;
> In every change, He faithful will remain.
> Be still, my soul: thy best, thy heavenly Friend
> Through thorny ways leads to a joyful end.
> Be still, my soul: thy God doth undertake

To guide the future, as He has the past.
Thy hope, thy confidence let nothing shake;
All now mysterious shall be bright at last.
Be still, my soul: the waves and winds still know
His voice Who ruled them while He dwelt below.[7]

In silence and solitude we develop a profound confidence in God's order and providence in our lives. In silence and solitude we see ourselves truly—we rejoice in the good God created in us, and we sense conviction for sins we need to confess. In silence we hear God's voice. Through silence and solitude we realize that ultimately we are never, ever alone.

talk about it

Discuss these questions with a friend or a small group of other moms.

1. When have you experienced silence or solitude as a negative thing, leading to feelings of isolation or depression? Why was it a negative experience?

2. Why do we often feel discomfort with silence or solitude? How might that discomfort be overcome?

3. When have you had a positive experience of silence or solitude? What made it a positive experience? How did it impact your relationship with God?

4. What do you think is a reasonable amount of quietness or alone time for your children? for yourself?

5. Which idea for weaving silence and solitude into your life appeals to you most? Why? What other ideas do you have?

try it

Here are ten ideas you can try.

1. Read these Scripture passages about silence and solitude: Psalm 4:4 and 37:7; Matthew 4:1–11; Mark 1:35; Luke 5:16 and 6:12. What do they teach about one's motivation for spending time in silence or solitude? How do your motivations line up with these verses? Journal your thoughts.

2. Wake up fifteen minutes earlier each day for one week. Sit in a comfortable chair and be still. Don't worry about your day. Don't pray with words. Just quiet your heart before God and wait in his presence.

3. Invite a friend to make a babysitting trade—you watch her kids for a few hours one day, and she watches yours another day. When it's your turn to be alone, go on an adventure of silence.

4. Utilize your time in the shower as a moment of sanity, serenity, and silence with God.

5. Sing (or read) the hymn "Be Still, My Soul" by Katharina A. von Schlegel. Then meditate on a line from the lyrics that stands out to you.

6. Take your kids on a walk for some cloud gazing, and bring along a picnic blanket. Don't set an agenda—just take your time, letting them run and play, doze in the stroller, or talk with you.

7. Establish a daily routine of quiet time for your kids and yourself. Allow kids to read or play in their room while you take a moment to breathe and be with God.

8. Limit the media consumption in your home by putting some guidelines into place or committing to a time of focused fasting from electronic media.

39

9. When you are alone in the car, turn off the radio and dedicate the time to God. Sit in his presence and still your heart before him.

10. Commit a day to communication with God by eliminating contact with the outside world. Turn on the answering machine instead of taking phone calls (unless they are emergencies). Don't check e-mail for a day. Set the snail mail aside. Talk to God in your heart about the day's experiences. (Be sure to communicate with your kids, though. They will still need it!)

3

scriptural learning

For the first few years of her life as a mom, Rachel worked in the corporate world of downtown Chicago. Balancing home life, work, and spiritual growth was a challenge, but there was one saving grace in her hectic routine: the hour-long train ride to and from her house in the burbs. Rachel explained, "I had time set aside for prayer, Bible reading, and reflection built right into my life, Monday through Friday." With nothing to distract her, Rachel's dreary commute was transformed into an intimate meeting with God.

Then came baby number two. "I quit working after my second pregnancy," Rachel said, "and I found out that time didn't work the same way. It's much harder to find free time to study or read the Bible now that I stay at home." This really surprised the twentysomething mother, who thought she'd be able to squeeze in Bible study during her kids' nap times. "But *I* often need the naps now. And I seldom want to attend a Sunday school class or Bible study when it requires leaving my children in the nursery or with a babysitter." Unless your children sleep an inordinate amount of time, you've likely faced the same dilemma: Parenting kids who need your attention while simultaneously trying to dig in deep to Scripture feels quintessentially impossible.

The spiritual discipline of study, at its very core, requires time, focus, and the absence of distractions—three assets most moms just don't have. Yet when we aren't plugged in to the Bible, we pay a spiritual price. As one friend put it, "When I am not spending enough time in the Word, I find myself wanting to go to church less. I find myself worrying about things more, like finances and time. I find that I have a shorter tolerance level with my children and my husband. I start viewing life through the wrong set of glasses." Another mom explained candidly, "When I am not in God's Word, I can feel myself becoming spiritually thirsty. And the tyranny of the urgent seems even *more* urgent with an infant on my hands. I've gone from drinking deeply from God's Word to taking a rushed gulp just to get me through the day."

> [E]xcessive busyness creates a disconnect with God...[It] quenches the Spirit and renders God a haunting stranger.
>
> —Bruce Demarest

soaking up scripture

We've been taught all our Christian lives that scriptural learning is important; we know that studying the Bible is something we *should* do, though it's something fewer than half of us actually do on a weekly basis.[1] But let's step back for a moment and explore *why* studying Scripture is important to spiritual growth. When questioned by a Pharisee about the greatest commandment in Scripture, Jesus answered him, "Love the Lord your God with all your heart and with all your soul and with all your mind and with all your strength" (Mark 12:30). *This* is why we read, study, and engage with God's Word. With our hearts, we respond to God's invitations to grow and change. Our souls are compelled, convicted, and empowered by the Holy Spirit as we digest Holy Scripture. Our minds are engaged in questioning, researching, and exploring the Bible. (Sometimes it just feels so good to get those rusty wheels in the brain turning again!) And with our strength— both emotional fortitude and physical effort—we defy laziness, sleepiness, hard times, or any other barriers from muting our love for God. We move beyond the guilt of "I know I *should*, but . . ." to raw, authentic passion for God's Word.

43

Through practicing the discipline of scriptural learning, we

Discover God. Exploring the Bible helps us find out who God is and what God is like.

Understand Ourselves. Through Scripture we come to know better who we are, both as individuals and as members of the human race.

Learn about Relationship with God. The Bible teaches us what our relationship with God is and what it can become. We observe how God has related to his people throughout history. We hear God speaking to us today. We're faced with God's expectations for us. We're presented with warnings, cautions, and guidance from God for daily living. We encounter and take confidence in God's promises to us.

> Oh, how I love your law! . . .
> How sweet are your words
> to my taste, sweeter than
> honey to my mouth!
>
> —Psalm 119: 97, 103

There are very few biblical examples of Scripture study in the sense that Christians practice it today—reading the Bible, taking notes, and consulting commentaries. In the ancient world, the average person simply didn't have a personal copy of Scripture to read and examine. But adolescent Jesus is a fabulous model for what we seek to do through the discipline of scriptural learning. Luke

2:41–52 records an incident in which Mary and Joseph realized their twelve-year-old son was missing. They eventually found him in the Temple, interacting with the teachers and priests. In a world where books were rare and access to them limited, these men were the keepers of the Scriptures, the teachers of God's Word. Luke described Jesus as "sitting among the teachers, listening to them and asking them questions. Everyone who heard him was amazed at his understanding and his answers" (verses 46–47). Granted, we'll never achieve Jesus' level of understanding regarding the Scriptures. But we can listen to God's Word and ask questions of what we find there with the goal of understanding God and God's message for us. That is the essence of scriptural learning.

putting it into action: mom-friendly ideas

Through this spiritual discipline, we make ourselves like a sponge—we immerse ourselves in God's Word, soak up his truth, and are filled within. Scriptural learning is an absolute essential for Christian growth—not just for you, but for your kids too! But if regular practices of scriptural learning aren't a part of your life right now, don't worry—they can be. Here are several tools you can use to build a firm foundation for daily living based on God's Word.

maximizing sermon impact

Is listening to the Sunday morning sermon pretty much your only channel for Scripture intake? If so, you're not alone. Many busy moms begin the week with the best intention to dive into God's Word on their own; but time slips away before they know it, and they find themselves in the pew again on Sunday morning, never having cracked open their Bibles in the past seven days. If this describes you, let's get one thing straight: Listening to good biblical teaching is an awesome way to practice the discipline of scriptural learning. So don't beat yourself up if this is the only Bible intake you've had so far. Instead, consider building on that solid base using the MSI principle—Maximize Sermon Impact. To practice the MSI principle, you'll need just two fifteen-minute blocks of time per week, a Bible, and a notebook.

The first step is to find out what one of the main biblical texts for next week's sermon will be (one easy way to find out is to call or e-mail your pastor). Then set aside about fifteen minutes toward the end of the week to read that Bible passage. As you read it, write down your questions or observations about the text. Then pray, asking God to teach you through the sermon on Sunday morning. If time gets away from you during the week, you could even do this late on Saturday night, right before bed!

45

Next, attentively listen to the sermon, taking notes in your notebook if you care to.

Finally, set aside fifteen more minutes of focused time early in the following week to reread the Scripture passage. Pray and jot notes, reflecting on what you learned and how God spoke to you through his Word and through the pastor. Be sure to write down any specific ways the Holy Spirit is prompting you to grow or change as a result of what you've learned.

Though thirty minutes a week may not seem like a lot of time, if you're currently in a season of life when you aren't spending any time in independent scriptural learning, this is a great place to start. Your focused efforts will bring the Sunday morning sermon to life!

scripture feasts

Have you ever begun reading a new novel late at night during an exhausting week? You read a few paragraphs and then conk out. The next night, you try to pick up where you left off only to discover you don't remember anything you read the night before. You decide to start over; but after a few minutes, your tired brain shuts off again and you're fast asleep. The next night you try one more time, but your lack of connection with the characters and plot has dulled your enthusiasm. You set the book on the nightstand and decide it might be better just to close your eyes and get some rest.

Spending time each day studying God's Word is an awesome avenue for spiritual growth. But—let's be honest about this—just as it is difficult to read a novel in five-minute chunks, it's impossible to study anything effectively in a five- or ten-minute bite of time with a crying baby in the background and a three-year-old launching Matchbox cars off your foot. Effective Bible study requires a significant span of uninterrupted, focused time.

Now brace yourself, because what I'm about to say might be considered borderline heretical: I believe that a weekly one-hour "feast" of time spent in in-depth study (or a biweekly or even monthly time, if that's all that's available) is far more preferable and measurably more effective than are five- or ten-minute daily cram sessions. Why? When we try to pack study into a miniscule bit of time, in an environment that is cluttered with distractions, we aren't really studying! Very little spiritual meaning can be drawn from such so-called study experiences. Glancing at Scripture for a few minutes a day is like skipping a rock over the surface of a lake. Scriptural study is like plumbing the water's depths.

So rather than trying to get up a few minutes early every day in order to study the Word—and invariably failing, feeling guilty, and quitting altogether—give yourself the freedom to identify and focus on Scripture feast times that are spread out over a realistic time frame. Your feast times will need to be kid free, so plan on getting up early, staying up late, or recruiting your husband or a friend to watch the kids so you can spend time with God.

During a feast time there are many different methods of study you could choose from. Here are a few (for specific books and study guides, see the Resources section of this book).

* Use a published Bible study guide.

* Read an entire short book of the Bible in one sitting, such as Ruth, Jonah, or one of the Epistles.

* Examine a text by recording your observations and questions, then supplementing your reading with a Bible commentary.

* Take notes on what you read, making observations, and drawing symbols directly on the pages of your Bible.

* Use Bible study tools such as a concordance (to study several scriptural uses of the same word) or a Bible dictionary (to learn the historical context or meaning of certain terms).

47

The method of study you select is not nearly as important as the fact that you are taking time to feast on God's Word. Use whatever method will enable you to create a meaningful time of exploration and scriptural learning, a precious time set aside to love God with your mind.

devotional reading

Perhaps you can't realistically set aside a significant block of time for feasting on God's Word. Or maybe you can, but you'd like to supplement your diet with a few Scripture snacks. In that case, consider spending five- or ten-minute blocks of time on devotional reading. Devotional reading is simply reading a short section of the Bible with a prayerful attitude. With regular exposure to our hearts in this manner, God's Word seeps in through osmosis, affecting our minds and actions without our realizing it. For your devotional reading, you could select a book of the Bible and read a chapter per day, or you could focus on the same text for several days in a row, spending time each day reflecting on what you've read.

In the rich history of the Church, we find two ancient methods of devotional reading that can be extremely powerful in our spiritual formation. Either can be done in just a small block of time. The first is called *lectio divina*.

Lectio Divina. Latin for "divine reading," this method of exploring Scripture is less cerebral than study but can lead to new understanding. In essence, it is the listening part of scriptural learning. But instead of auditory listening, it is listening with the heart. In the practice of lectio divina, you focus on a small portion of Scripture and read it meditatively, seeking God's Word to you in the Holy Word. Lectio divina can be practiced by simply rereading a short text several times, emphasizing different words and contemplating what they mean. A broader experience of lectio divina traditionally involves the following five parts:

If you've never tried lectio divina before, here are some passages with which you may want to start: Psalm 61:3–4, 84:10–12; Micah 6:8; Ephesians 1:7–9, 5:1–2; Philippians 2:5–8; or 1 John 1:5–7.

1. *Silencio* (Silence). Take a moment to still your heart and mind and focus on God's presence.

2. *Lectio* (Reading). Read the text silently or aloud, slowing down, rereading, and emphasizing different words.

3. *Meditato* (Meditation). Meditate on the text, reflecting on whatever stands out to you and allowing it to soak in.

4. *Oratio* (Prayer). Pray about what you've read and considered, declaring your thoughts and feelings about the text to God and listening to his promptings.

5. *Contemplatio* (Contemplation). Quietly wait on God and focus on his presence.

In a basic sense, lectio divina is a method of integrating the discipline of scriptural learning with the disciplines of prayer and meditation.

Contemplative Reading. The second ancient method of devotional reading that can be especially meaningful to busy moms is contemplative reading. This method was developed by Ignatius of Loyola as part of the Spiritual Exercises he created between 1522 and 1524. Contemplative reading is simply using your imagination when reading Scripture (especially the Gospels). It is stepping into a story about Jesus and considering what it would have been like to have been there, observing Jesus' actions and hearing his words.

Contemplative reading, like lectio divina, is done in five steps:

1. Select and read a Gospel passage.

2. Begin praying in your usual manner.

3. Ask God specifically to help you open your heart and guide your thoughts as you "step inside" the passage.

4. Use your imagination to actively place yourself in the scene, either as an observer or as one of the people who interacted with Jesus. Consider what it might have felt like, looked like, sounded like, and smelled like to be there. Imagine the scenery, the weather, or who else might have been nearby. Now think through the event or teaching described in the passage. What is Jesus' tone of voice? What is the impact of his words or actions on those around you? on you? What is it like to be there with Jesus?

5. Respond to Jesus—talk to him and listen to his response in your heart. Ignatius described what he did during this step as

If you'd like to try the practice of Ignatian contemplative reading, here are some texts with which you may want to start: Matthew 27:27–50; Mark 5:21–42; Luke 7:36–47; John 13:1–17, John 20:19–29.

••••••••••••••••••••••••••••••

talking to Jesus "as one friend speaks to another."[2]

Through using the God-given gift of imagination in contemplative reading, we get to know Jesus better. We allow the text to come to life in our minds. We are powerfully reminded of the reality of the Incarnation and

become aware that Jesus, the Word, is more than just words printed on paper. We grow to know Jesus better in a three-dimensional way.

scripture memorization

Memorizing Scripture—or memorizing anything, for that matter—has never come easily to me. When I became a teenager and graduated from our church's midweek children's program, I felt liberated from the regimen of Bible memorization and decided that I would never again have need to commit verses of Scripture to memory. The practice didn't seem helpful to me spiritually, and it reminded me of being forced to memorize facts and dates in history class. Unfortunately, I had missed the real purpose behind Scripture memorization. It isn't an achievement, done in order to impress others; and it isn't intended to simply store Bible data on the hard drive of our minds. It is a way of internalizing Scripture so that we can meditate on it.

I was inspired to recover the discipline of Scripture memorization by my friend Julie, a mother of three, who also works part time. Julie's attitude toward Scripture memorization is a one-eighty from what mine was. "Bible memory has been a huge part of my life," she said. "It helps me stay focused even when life around me is seemingly falling apart." Through memorizing Scripture, busy moms, who have limited time to sit down and read the Bible, can meditate on God's truth anywhere: in front of the copy machine at work, in line at the grocery store, mowing the lawn, or working out. We can think about and reflect on God's peace and comfort, his character, his truth. Like a jar filled up with jewels, we can store up God's Word in our hearts. (See Psalm 119:11 ESV.)

And memorizing Scripture isn't beneficial only to you—this is something you can get kids (even infants!) involved in. Julie has turned Scripture memorization into a daily spiritual growth practice for her entire family: "Since the children were very young, I have been reciting a passage of Scripture to them at night before they go to bed. At one point I had my four-year-old and two-year-old hopping around the room reciting Psalm 23. They have already learned several verses. Whatever I am memorizing, I do it aloud; and they always learn it."

If you are like me and your mind isn't geared toward memorization, don't be intimidated by this discipline. Begin with the simple practice of writing the passage on an index card. You might also jot down pneumonic devices like pictures and symbols to help you remember the passage. Take the card with you, and try to read it to yourself at least once a day. Then commit to reading it to your kids as you tuck them in to bed at night. The cumulative effect of reading the same passage twice a day will eventually embed the verses in your mind. You will have memorized them before you know it. It really works!

storytelling

One of the easiest and most fun ways to grow in scriptural learning is to tell Bible stories to your kids. There are lots of great Christian children's books out there that can guide you in storytelling, but even better is the challenge of reading the text then retelling the story yourself. Why? Because this causes you to explore the story in a new way as you are forced to answer these questions:

- What are the key points?
- What truth is the text emphasizing?
- What can my children learn from this?
- What will I emphasize as I tell this story to them?

Your kids will love the special attention they receive from you during storytelling times, and they'll get to know God's Word in the process. As you tell your children Bible stories, you can rev up the storytelling process by using different voices, dramatic facial expressions, dolls, puppets, or props. You will help to create a long-term impact on your kids by reminding them of truths from the stories during everyday interactions if you say things like "God wants you to obey just like Noah did" or "You can have courage and be brave just like David was when he fought Goliath." Once your kids have heard several stories, they'll start requesting encore performances of their favorites.

filling in the holes

Remember Rachel, my friend who was settling in to life as a stay-at-home mom? Rachel gave me some input for this book by filling out a personal evaluation just like the one you filled out in the Try It section of chapter 1. God used the evaluation process to help Rachel identify the specific ways in which she hopes to grow. She explained,

Answering these questions led me to a place of deeper introspection about my own habits. I realized that I was yearning for the use of my brain in study, for more of the Word in my life, and for mentoring from someone else. Then out of the blue last Sunday, a friend invited me to a women's Bible study that provides childcare. This was an easy way to fill in the "holes" in my spiritual life—so I joined that Bible study group yesterday. I am really looking forward to this new opportunity for growth. I already feel blessed by it!

How about you? Is scriptural learning a hole in your spiritual life? If so, how can you fill it? Take an honest look at your daily routine and determine what step you can take to integrate scriptural learning into it. Determine to say with the psalmist,

I will meditate on your precepts and fix my eyes on your ways. I will delight in your statutes; I will not forget your word. . . . Teach me, O LORD, the way of your statutes; and I will keep it to the end. Give me understanding, that I may keep your law and observe it with my whole heart. Lead me in the path of your commandments, for I delight in it. Incline my heart to your testimonies. (Ps. 119:15–16, 33–36 ESV)

talk about it

Discuss these questions with a friend or a small group of other moms.

1. Has there been a time in your life when you have had a positive, impactful experience of spending time in God's Word? Describe it.
2. What is your favorite Bible verse or passage? Why is it meaningful to you? How has God spoken to you through it?
3. We know that we should be immersed in Scripture—but why? In your own words, describe why you think the discipline of scriptural learning is important.

4. Which of the approaches to scriptural learning described in this chapter appeals to you most? Why?

5. How can you share scriptural learning experiences with your kids? Be creative!

try it

Here are ten ideas you can try.

1. Read these passages about scriptural learning: Deuteronomy 6:4–9, 8:3; Joshua 1:8; Psalm 119:1–5, 10–11; and 2 Timothy 3:14–17. What inspires you? What convicts you? Journal your thoughts.

2. Identify a time during the next two weeks for a Scripture feast, during which you can study God's Word for one or two hours. (Arrange for someone to watch your kids, or set aside time early in the morning or late at night when they're asleep.)

3. Spend time each day this week reading a portion of Psalm 119, then reflecting on the reasons why you love God's Word.

4. Find out what biblical texts will be the focus of next week's sermon. Then try out the MSI principle.

5. Read an Old Testament story or a New Testament parable. Then shine up your storytelling (or puppeteering) skills and retell it to your kids.

6. From Sunday's sermon or from your personal devotional reading, select a Bible passage you want to memorize, and then commit yourself to reading or reciting it to each of your children every night for a week.

7. Try out lectio divina by reading and meditating on a short passage of Scripture several times during the upcoming week.

8. If your kids are old enough to use a crayon (without eating it), invite them to help you create Bible verse flashcards to aid in memorization. For example, draw images of fruit on index cards and invite your kids to color them for you. Label each fruit with one of the fruit of the Spirit (Gal. 5:22–23) and talk with your kids about what they mean.

9. Dust off your imagination and spend some time in Ignatian contemplative reading this week. Commit to spending ten minutes or more (alone) doing this.

55

10. Figure out one way you can connect with others through the discipline of scriptural learning—such as joining a women's Bible study (with childcare), a small group Bible study for families, or a MOPS (Mothers of Preschoolers) group. You'll be amazed at how refreshing it is to study God's Word with other adults, free from any distractions from your kids!

4

prayer and meditation

M odern science has enabled us to discover amazing things about the miracle of fetal development. By the end of a mother's third month of pregnancy, her growing baby has already developed the ability to smell. By the sixth month, the little one is able to hear. And by the end of the seventh month, the baby's sense of taste has developed, his sense of touch enables him to respond to pain, and his growing sense of sight causes his eyes to respond to light.[1]

But there's one discovery doctors haven't made yet—though I'm sure in no time it will be verified with hard science. From the very moment of birth, infants appear to have a fully developed MTTP sensory ability. My new baby, Lucia, excels in her use of MTTP, and I know from anecdotal evidence that every single one of my friends' kids also has a very active MTTP sense. I'm *certain* your child has the same.

MTTP is that radar-like ability which enables children to know that Mom's Trying To Pray. As soon as their MTTP sensor alerts the brain, they immediately respond with crying, demands, fights, hunger, whining, or daredevil mischief. It never fails—almost any time a busy mom sits down for a much-needed, focused, extended time of prayer, *Beep! Beep! Beep!* The MTTP sensor sounds in the child's brain, and crying, misbehavior, or some other stressful interruption immediately ensues. MTTP sensors must have been one of the unmentioned consequences of that first sin in Eden!

wanted: more time, more prayer 57

Many of us struggle with prayer. We struggle with the disconnect between saying, "I'll pray for you" and actually praying. We have any number of excuses for why we don't pray. We're too busy. We're too distracted. We mean to pray, but forget. And this struggle is intensified by motherhood when the number of "excuses" for prayerlessness doubles, triples, or even quadruples!

Yet in motherhood, our need for prayer also multiplies. Suddenly we are given the startling responsibility of caring for another precious human being. Along with that responsibility come worries, demands, questions, and concerns, all of which we can bring before the Lord in prayer. In fact, many mothers have found that though they now have less time available for prayer, parenting has deepened their desire for prayer in a surprising way. Jennifer, a new mom, told me, "Having my son increased my dependency on God, my trust in him, and my reliance on him. Many times I've thought, *I don't know how to do this!* Being a mom has pushed me to turn to God in my weakness." As we face this contradiction between our increased need for prayer and shrinking allotment of time for prayer, what are we to do?

Though there are certainly some "prayer warrior" moms out there who wake up early each morning to spend an hour or two in focused, attentive prayer or meditation, for most mothers of young kids the idea of spending extended, uninterrupted time in prayer sounds like a dream. And when it comes to meditation, well, forget about it! Christian meditation has been practiced by monks, nuns, hermits, and ascetics since ancient times—but none of those people had kids! In fact, many of the great teachers of Christian meditation had virtually no responsibilities other than silently focusing on God. Some never even saw another human being for years at a time!

Though these ways of practicing prayer and meditation are admirable, they're pretty much incompatible with the life of a busy, exhausted mother of young children. So let's start by taking a new look at what prayer and meditation really are and considering what they could look like in this season of life.

a fresh glimpse at prayer and meditation

In its most basic sense, prayer is speaking to God. In prayer, we can speak praises, confessions, requests, thanks, questions, doubts, and random thoughts. Prayer can be practiced in specific windows of time but also as a constant, ongoing conversation with God throughout the day.

> Whole prayer grows into the wholeness of divine relationship.
>
> —Walter Wangerin Jr.

Meditation is essentially prayerful listening to God. Thomas Merton described it this way: "[Meditation] teaches you how to become aware of the presence of God; and most of all it aims at bringing you to a state of almost constant loving attention to God, and dependence on Him. The real purpose of meditation is . . . [to] enter into a conscious and loving contact with God."[2] In meditation, we set aside words in order to focus our thoughts and attentions on God, on God's qualities, on God's Word, or on God's world. There are many avenues of Christian meditation, including some practices we've already explored, such as intentionally quieting the heart, observing God's qualities in nature, lectio divina, and pondering memorized Scriptures. In all its various forms, meditation is essentially "a tranquil listening of the heart, that allows God to enter through all its doors and passages."[3]

These twin practices of prayer and meditation—the cycle of speaking and soul listening—function together to foster and strengthen our intimacy with God. C. S. Lewis emphasized this relational focus of prayer, clarifying that prayer is meant to be much more than simply naming requests to God: "Prayer in the sense of petition, asking for things, is a small part of it; confession and penitence are its threshold, adoration its sanctuary, the presence and vision and enjoyment of God its bread and wine. In it God shows Himself to us."[4] In prayer and meditation, just as in human relationships, we come to know God better through speaking and listening. And through the very act of praying, we assert something powerful: God is, God loves, God hears, and God speaks.

putting it into action: mom-friendly ideas

Though your opportunities for long stretches of uninterrupted, focused times of prayer and meditation will be rare, your prayer life need not be any less powerful than a prayer warrior who spends hours a day in prayer. In fact, God can use the hectic reality of your minute-to-minute life as a mom to give you an entirely new perspective on what prayer and meditation really are and how they can be woven into every moment of your life! Here are some ideas to help you integrate prayer and soul listening into the nitty-gritty of your life.

practice god's presence

In the 1600s, a humble monk named Brother Lawrence worked as the dishwasher and cook for his monastery. Though he enjoyed the monastery's routine, which included time set aside each day for private prayer and devotions, he found that he didn't get much out of it. Instead, Brother Lawrence discovered that he best experienced intimacy and communion with God when he was up to his elbows in murky water and dirty dishes. In other words, it was in the stuff of real life that he felt God's presence—not in special times set aside for "spiritual" purposes. In a letter to his friend Joseph de Beaufort, Brother Lawrence explained how he made it a practice to "pray continually" (1 Thess. 5:17) by giving attention to God's steady company: "I make it my business only to persevere in His holy presence . . . [in] an habitual, silent, and secret conversation of the soul with God. . . . My most usual method is this simple attention, and such a general passionate regard to God."[5] Brother Lawrence felt strongly that "it was a great delusion to think that the times of prayer ought to differ from other times."[6]

Picture for a moment what it might be like to live as a "Mother Lawrence." Constant communion with God through changing diapers, wiping runny noses, cleaning toys, disciplining children, and dealing with continual interruptions—could it be possible?

Yes.

This practice of God's presence isn't about doing anything outwardly; it's simply a refocusing of our inner perspective. My friend Amie describes her mind-set shift this way:

I used to think that God wanted us to pencil him in—that he was as linear and Western minded as myself and that he was really much more pleased when I had "prayer time" and "Scripture-reading time" and had my life sufficiently organized so that as long as he occupied a certain percentage of my day planner he was appeased and all was well. But *he* breaks in like a crying child. *He* is in the interruption. He shows me that he is always there—on the subway, while I am changing a diaper, in the supermarket, behind the window where the widow sits alone. And whether I choose to acknowledge him or not is up to me.

Amie has zeroed in on the foundational idea of practicing God's presence: recognizing the truth that as a result of our salvation, God's presence is *continually* with us. We simply need to attentively focus on this truth and not lose sight of it even in the midst of interruptions and distractions. Though outward demands of work or home can draw our minds away from God, "It is the *heart* . . . whose attention we must carefully focus on God."[7] Developing this mind-set (maybe *heart-set* would be a better term) requires effort on our part as we constantly remind ourselves that God is here, God sees my life, God hears my heart, and God knows my needs.

> "And surely I am with you always, to the very end of the age."
> —Matthew 28:20

61

God doesn't require that our prayers be well formulated or profound; God doesn't mind if on some days 99 percent of our conversation with him is made up of SOS prayers: "God, help!" In the presence of our loving God, we can be real. Our conversation with God can be as simple as speaking phrases to God like these:

- I feel stressed right now. God, please help me to calm down.
- Thanks for my son, God. He's adorable!
- Potty training drives me crazy! God, show me how to help my child learn this.

Our listening to God may consist of hearing answers from God through promptings in our hearts and minds; being reminded of God's love and promises through people and circumstances; specific phrases from Scripture popping into our heads; or simply through sensing God's continual, loving presence.

Of all the spiritual disciplines that are part of the renovation process, praying by practicing God's presence is one of the simplest to begin. As my friend Becky (a mom of two kids under three) described, "Prayer is probably the most significant part of my growth as a mom. I call, and God responds over and over again. And it's one of the easiest of the disciplines to participate in—in the heat of the moment, on the run, in the dark, when I'm tired. Prayer doesn't require a lot of preparation, so it fits well with the rhythms of motherhood."

pray for and with your kids

Perhaps the greatest privilege and the most sobering responsibility of motherhood is to pray for our kids. Praying for children was something our Savior took very seriously: "Then little children were brought to Jesus for him to place his hands on them and *pray* for them. But the disciples rebuked those who brought them. Jesus said, 'Let the little children come to me, and do not hinder them, for the kingdom of heaven belongs to such as these'" (Matt. 19:13–14, emphasis added). As Jesus did, we can pray for our children, blessing them and laying hands on them in love. We can dedicate their lives to God. We can intercede on their behalf, bringing their needs to God in words they cannot yet utter or understand. And most important, we can seek for them to know Jesus personally and grow in faith throughout their lives. We can pray for them as Paul did for the Philippians:

And this is my prayer: that your love may abound more and more in knowledge and depth of insight, so that you may be able to discern what is best and may be pure and blame-less until the day of Christ, filled with the fruit of righteousness that comes through Jesus Christ—to the glory and praise of God. (Phil. 1:9–11)

One mom I know writes a prayer for her daughter in a journal once or twice a week. Another friend, a mother of four kids all under five years old, makes a nightly habit of sneaking into her kids' rooms once they've fallen asleep and gently laying her hand on each of her children's heads, thanking God for them and praying about her hopes for each of them. She prays for their growing faith, for their future jobs or marriages, and for their daily growth. As my friend gazes at her children's sleeping faces—when even her oldest looks once again so like she did as a newborn—this mother is filled with gratitude and joy at these living gifts God has given her. The frustrations of the day slip away as she is reminded again that the privilege of being a mother is worth its many demands.

In addition to praying *for* our kids, praying *with* our children is also important. This is one of the most important ways we can help them develop spiritual growth habits. The approach taken in pray-ing with children will vary from family to family. Here are some ideas you might try:

- Pray grace together before meals.
- Recite memorized children's prayers at bedtime.
- Prompt your child to say, "Thanks, God" each night for var-ious things that happened throughout the day.
- Sing simple songs and hymns of prayer and praise together, such as "For the Beauty of the Earth" or "I Love You, Lord."
- Pray Scripture passages together, such as the Lord's Prayer.

You can also help your children learn to practice God's presence by praying spontaneously and out loud about simple things; your kids will pick up on the habit and will soon start doing it themselves. One friend shared with me what happened soon after she began speaking short prayers aloud in front of her daughter.

Now she has begun to mimic my habits. What a blessing it was when my three-year-old shouted, "Thanks, God!" when her daddy pulled into a parking space near the front of a restaurant. Daddy was curious and amused the first time this happened, and I had to explain that I often pray aloud for a good parking space to make it easier moving two little ones in and out of a store. God has answered those prayers many times, and I always try to thank him on the spot. Now my daughter spontaneously (and vocally) thanks God for little things throughout the day!

As you pray with and for your children, you're doing much more than setting an important example they can follow—you're teaching them the secret to a healthy spiritual life and helping them recognize God as the author of all good things.

meditate on motherhood

Nursing moms often find themselves feeling severely limited in their efforts to pursue spiritual growth. They cannot sleep through the night, they cannot sit through a church service, they can't participate in a small group Bible study without having to step aside to breastfeed. Yet even in this seemingly isolated aspect of motherhood God can reveal himself to us. My friend Angela was in the throes of those first shocking months of motherhood, feeling that her life had been turned upside down by the constant demands of her new son. Yet one night when she was nursing, God broke through. As she was looking at her son, she began to think about nursing and what it revealed to her about God. She considered that just as her son physically relied on her for sustenance, she must rely on God to sustain her and provide for her needs. As she thought about her deep love for her son and the joy she feels in caring for him, she considered the depth of God's love for his children and his delight in being our ultimate Provider and Protector. In that quiet, lonely, late-night moment, she found herself in the middle of a moving experience of meditation. As Thomas Merton put it, she was immersed in "loving contact with God."

65

In the very stuff of motherhood, we can find deep truths about God that serve as prompts for meaningful meditation. As we hold or care for our little ones, we can meditate on God's comfort, love, and care for us. As we bathe our kids, we can prayerfully consider how God "washes away" our sins, or we can recall our baptism and its meaning in our lives. As we prepare meals and feed our children, we can focus on the many forms of nourishment God provides to us. Even the horrid task of changing diapers can help us contemplate the theological truth that though we are helpless and stranded in our cruddy sins and their consequences, Jesus has rescued us from that situation, cleansing us, and helping us start afresh.

breathing deep

Have you ever felt as if you just need some space and time to breathe? One important form of prayer that has been practiced by Christians since ancient times is called "breath" prayer. It is the practice of praying a short, memorized prayer by silently saying one phrase as you breathe in, then

> [B]reath prayer reminds us that . . . God is the oxygen of our soul, and we need to breathe him in all day long.
>
> —Adele Ahlberg Calhoun

praying the next phrase as you breathe out. One of the best-known breath prayers is called the Jesus Prayer. It is drawn from the words of blind Bartimaeus in Mark 10:47 and of the tax collector in Jesus' parable in Luke 18:13. The Jesus Prayer is basic, sincere, and to the point:

Jesus,
Son of David,
have mercy on me,
a sinner.

You can draw from other short Scripture passages for breath prayer, such as the following:

- "May the words of my mouth and the meditation of my heart be pleasing in your sight" (Ps. 19:14).
- You are my refuge and strength, an ever-present help in trouble (based on Ps. 46:1).
- "You are the Christ, the Son of the living God" (Matt. 16:16).
- "Holy, holy, holy is the Lord God Almighty, who was, and is, and is to come" (Rev. 4:8).

The goal of breath prayer is to form a habitual, internal cadence of prayer. This isn't mindless prayer; it is ongoing, basic prayer that ushers you into an attitude of meditation, with your soul calmed, poised, and attentive toward God.

Two of the best times of day for busy moms to pray in this manner are when waking in the morning and when falling asleep at night. If you like to hit the snooze button at least once when your alarm goes off in the morning, try to focus your heart on soul listening by praying a simple breath prayer during those warm, restful few minutes before the alarm sounds again and the day begins. And instead of letting worries and concerns wreak havoc in your mind as you try to fall asleep at night, focus on resting in God's presence as you pray a breath prayer while falling asleep. It's much more meaningful than trying to count sheep!

redefining success in prayer

There will come a season in your life when it is again possible to set aside lengthy blocks of time for focused prayer and Christian meditation. Yet in the meantime, your prayer life doesn't have to be on hold; it can flourish. For busy moms, growth in prayer and meditation often comes down to readjusting the way we define a successful prayer life, both for ourselves and for our kids.

Carolyn, a pastor's wife with three young kids, related this story to me: "When it comes to family prayer time, we just do what we can. If the kids are not into it, we move on. Last night during devotions, we were ready to pray. When I started the prayer, the kids got the giggles. I could have been strict and made them stop, but God enjoys their laughter, so I giggled along until they were ready to thank God for their blankies and toys and friends that day."

Prayer isn't about somberness, seriousness, or even necessarily spiritual depth—it's about being real before God as we grow in intimacy with him through speaking and soul listening. It's about the joys and giggles, the frustrations and busy schedules, the honest desires of our heart, all rolled into one ongoing, meaningful conversation with our ever-present God. It is "a personal contact between embryonic, incomplete persons (ourselves) and the utterly concrete Person."[8] Through prayer and meditation, you can "set your minds on things above" (Col. 3:2) and come to see God's presence in each moment of motherhood.

talk about it

Discuss these questions with a friend or a small group of other moms.

1. Do you struggle with finding time for prayer or meditation? What usually happens when you attempt to spend focused time on these disciplines?

2. What were your impressions of prayer and how it should be practiced before you read this chapter? What were your thoughts about Christian meditation?

3. How have the ideas in this chapter affected your understanding of the disciplines of prayer and meditation? What other thoughts do you have on the meaning and purpose of these disciplines?

4. Describe ways you pray as a family, such as bedtime prayers or grace before meals. What are some other ideas you have for helping your children experience intimacy with God through prayer?

5. Which of the ideas about prayer and meditation in this chapter do you most want to integrate into your life?

try it

Here are ten ideas you can try.

1. Explore these biblical teachings on prayer and meditation: Psalm 5:1–3, Matthew 6:5–15, Luke 18:1–14, Romans 8:26–27, Ephesians 6:18, and Philippians 4:8. Reflect on the personal insights these passages give you about your own prayer life, and journal your thoughts.

2. Write "God is present" on a card and post it somewhere in your house or your work area. Then several times throughout the day (such as at the start of each hour), focus your mind on this truth. As you refocus your awareness on God's presence, speak and listen to him in your heart.

3. Say at least one spontaneous prayer aloud in front of your kids each day, even if it's just one sentence about something small. You could invite your kids to join in by saying something like, "Let's tell God the things we love about him!"

4. Get up early one morning (or stay up late some night) so you can be alone, then grab a journal and write a heartfelt prayer for each of your children.

5. Sneak into your kids' rooms at night and pray over each of them individually. (Consider praying the text of Philippians 1:9–11.)

6. The psalmist meditated on God's Word and laws (Ps. 119:15, 23, 48, 78, 97, 99), God's love (48:9), God's works and wonders (77:12; 119:27; 143:5; 145:5), and God's promises (119:148). Read these passages, then spend time throughout the day meditating on one of these topics.

69

7. Cover the dinner table with newsprint paper. Each night at dinner, have family members share prayer requests and write (or draw) them on the tablecloth.

8. Post pictures of people and prayer needs on the fridge, then use them as visual prompts for family prayer at lunchtime.

9. Select a breath prayer to practice this week, either from the ideas listed on page 66 or from your own Scripture memorization.

10. Use a motherhood moment this week as an opportunity for meditation by focusing on spiritual truths as you bathe, feed, or clothe your child.

5

life change

You've had a hectic morning but somehow managed to make it out the door. You were able to get dressed in a cute outfit, fix your hair and makeup, nurse the baby, feed your toddler, pack everyone into the car and then drop them off at the babysitter's. You're meeting an old friend for coffee—someone you haven't seen since high school.

The mini-reunion goes well, in spite of a few naturally awkward moments. Afterward, you pick up the kids and drive home, feeling like your day (for once) is off to a great start! But as you arrive home, your eye catches something in the mirror in your entry hall. *Did I see that right?* you wonder. You take a few steps back and look at your reflection again. *Yup, I saw it right.* There's a four-inch cascade of dried baby spit-up on the front of your shirt, and you've got a huge smudge of lipstick in the center of your front teeth. *I can't believe this. . . .*

You had felt so good, so put together. But your hurried glance in the mirror on the way out the door somehow failed to bring these two embarrassing items to your attention. You *thought* you looked one way, but reality was humiliatingly different. Have you ever had a moment like this? I've had many—and they're always embarrassing. If it were only our physical appearance that we sometimes passed over too quickly, it wouldn't be so bad. But we are often too busy to realize that we do this same thing with our spiritual lives. The tyranny of the urgent—of the important, immediate responsibilities of motherhood—can force us into the habit of giving our spiritual life occasional glances instead of much-needed moments of looking in the mirror, making eye contact with ourselves, and seeing *reality*.

an honest look at your reflection

Intimately connected with scriptural learning and prayer are the responses of honest self-evaluation and life application—the discipline I call *life change*. James describes this discipline (or the need for it) this way:

> Be doers of the word, and not hearers only, deceiving yourselves. For if anyone is a hearer of the word and not a doer, he is like a man who looks intently at his natural face in a mirror. For he looks at himself and goes away and at once forgets what he was like. But the one who looks into the perfect law, the law of liberty, and perseveres, being no hearer who forgets but a doer who acts, he will be blessed in his doing. (James 1:22–25 ESV)

Life change is composed of the habits and practices that enable us to respond as doers of the promptings of the Holy Spirit, which are revealed through prayer and God's Word. Life change as a spiritual discipline is taking stock of our real, everyday life and taking action to apply God's Word and the Spirit's leading to our lives. The Bible is filled with portraits of life change, and one of the most memorable is that of Zacchaeus, the diminutive man with gargantuan courage. (See Luke 19:1–10.)

As Jesus passed through town, Zacchaeus—a chief tax collector, who had become rich through greed and dishonest gain—wanted to see Jesus. Zacchaeus was too short to see through the crowd, so he ran ahead and climbed a tree. When Jesus saw him, he spoke to him kindly, inviting himself to Zacchaeus's house. Zacchaeus responded to Jesus gladly, and almost immediately he publicly declared, "Look, Lord! Here and now I give half of my possessions to the poor, and if I have cheated anybody out of anything, I will pay back four times the amount" (verse 8). Jesus had hardly said anything to Zacchaeus—no poking or prodding to get Zacchaeus to evaluate the sin in his life. Instead, self-examination and life change were instant and instinctive responses when Zacchaeus interacted with Jesus, the Word of God made flesh.

your power source

American history provides us with another interesting portrait of life change. When Benjamin Franklin was in his early twenties, he decided to embark on an effort to achieve moral perfection. He began by creating a list of twelve virtues that he felt were important to put into practice in his daily life: temperance, silence, order, resolution, frugality, industry, sincerity, justice, moderation, cleanliness, tranquility, and chastity. A trusted Quaker friend of Franklin's suggested that he might also want to add humility to his list, for he had observed that Franklin had a bit of a problem with pride. So Franklin set about an active, methodical effort to embody his list of (now) thirteen virtues. He created a chart that listed the virtues vertically

73

and the days of the week horizontally. At the end of each day, Franklin evaluated his behavior, marking with a black dot each virtue he had failed to achieve. Soon he realized that thirteen items were too many to focus on each day, so he determined to examine one virtue each week and trust that he would do well in the others too. Franklin envisioned that after a week of intense focus, he would have mastered the first virtue and could move on to the second.[1]

74

In some ways Franklin's effort is a powerful example for us—he clearly took his daily living seriously and put significant, targeted effort into aligning his everyday behavior with his personal values. But Franklin eventually failed in his efforts; in fact, he lived the last years of his life as a womanizer, a glutton, and still lacked significantly in the humility department. Franklin's failure stems from one central problem: his efforts to reform his life were drawn solely from his own strength and will.

Franklin didn't recognize two important truths. First, we have a sin nature—a natural tendency to give up, screw up, rebel, fail, fight, and fall. No matter how hard we try, we can't overcome this tendency on our own. It will always come back to bite us. Second, Franklin—who famously discovered how to channel electricity—missed the mark when it came to the true power source for life change: God. Even our best-intended efforts to change our behavior will fail if we rely on our own power. When practicing life change, we must ask God's Spirit to channel *his* power through us so that we can accomplish changes we would never have the strength to make on our own.

In practicing the discipline of life change, we

- *Examine.* We look honestly at ourselves in the mirror of self-examination to rate our daily lives—not our *ideas* about living, but the way we actually live.

- *Respond.* We respond to the Holy Spirit's conviction that we receive through prayer or through God's Word.

- *Recognize.* We recognize and repent of our sins, shortcomings, and failings.

- *Reaffirm.* We reaffirm our reliance on God's Spirit to change and transform us.

- *Commit.* We commit to do our part by putting forth our best effort to live differently.

- *Act.* We seek to live out our true identity in Christ through specific actions or inner commitments.

- *Praise.* We praise God for the changes he is making in our lives.

75

the motherhood mirror

Everything changes when we have kids, and one of the most emotionally brutal changes that motherhood brings is the big, bold mirror it puts in our face. That mirror, reflecting our daily thoughts and actions back to us, often screams: *This is you! This is where you fall short. These are your faults and failings. Surprise! You ain't supermom!* My friend Stacy described her experience this way: "Becoming a mom has magnified the faults and struggles that I don't like to admit, and it has forced me to deal with them a bit more. It has shown me that I'm much more selfish than I ever wanted to believe! I don't like the fact that motherhood has revealed much of what I tried to ignore, but it's been good for me to try to acknowledge and address those areas in more depth."

> This is a call for us to reconsider how we have been approaching our life, in light of the fact that we now, in the presence of Jesus, have the option of living within the surrounding movements of God's eternal purposes, of taking our life into his life.
>
> —Dallas Willard

putting it into action: mom-friendly ideas

God speaks to us about our needs to grow and change through prayer and through his Word, but sometimes he speaks most loudly through our own precious children. As we look into their faces, as we respond to their needs, as we lose our patience or steam up with frustration over their behavior, we see clearly that we aren't perfect—not even *close*. We know we need to grow and change in order to be the best moms we can be, and we need God's help to do it. Our temptation at this point will be to wallow in crippling feelings of failure. Instead, we can put into action some meaningful mom-focused habits that cause life change to become a reality.

practice self-examination

"Search me, O God, and know my heart! Try me and know my thoughts! And see if there be any grievous way in me, and lead me in the way everlasting!" (Ps. 139:23–24 ESV). As we encounter God through silence, solitude, scriptural learning, prayer, and meditation, we naturally begin to echo the passionate desire of the psalmist: *God, speak to my heart and show me where to change. Point out my shortcomings and sins and show me how to live rightly!*

The problem is that we can begin to see the Holy Spirit like the antivirus software on our home computer. We believe that we can passively "hibernate" while God searches our hearts and motives, identifies problems, and then painlessly eliminates them. Unfortunately, the Christian life just doesn't work that way. We must actively participate in the search process. We need to have the courage to regularly face ourselves, take stock of both our behavior and our inner attitudes, and work alongside God to take action to change them.

Ignatius of Loyola taught that Jesus followers should regularly spend time in prayerful reflection, taking stock of their day and evaluating how well they lived out their faith. He called this practice *examen* and outlined it in five basic parts:

1. *Recognize* that you are in the presence of God.

2. *Reflect* on your day with gratitude and thank God for how he blessed you, guided you, and provided for you.

3. *Ask* the Holy Spirit to help you as you prepare to evaluate the outer actions and inner motives of your day. Open yourself to the Holy Spirit's leading.

77

4. *Review* your day prayerfully. Begin with the morning, and think through the events that occurred during the day. Consider your interactions with your children, spouse, and others; reflect on your inner thoughts and feelings; evaluate your use of time and your attentiveness to God. As you review your day, joyfully respond to the promptings of the Holy Spirit as God points out areas in which you fell short of how he wants you to live and to love.

5. *Reconcile* with God by confessing your shortcomings and receiving his forgiveness. Then resolve to do better tomorrow with God's help.

Many Christian teachers since Ignatius have recognized the importance of spiritual self-examination. John Wesley made this type of examination a central part of the Bible study meetings he led during the 1700s. During each meeting, participants honestly answered these questions: "What known sins have you committed since our last meeting? What temptations have you met with? How were you delivered? What have you thought, said, or done of which you doubt whether it be sin or not?"[2] You may want to follow Ignatius's pattern or use Wesley's questions as a guide, or you may want to construct a practice of examen on your own. The important thing is not the specific method of reflection and evaluation you choose but that you cultivate the habit of doing it.

Ignatius envisioned examen as thirty minutes of reflection; but if that doesn't fit the rhythm of your life, you could also practice it in five- or ten-minute periods as you get ready for bed or even as you're in bed. You could silently pray through examen, or you might journal your thoughts. You could even make a practice of thinking through examen at a halfway point during the day, perhaps when you're making peanut-butter-and-jelly sandwiches for the kids' lunch.

You can also impart the principle of examen to your kids by inviting them to reflect on their day during a short conversation as you tuck them in to bed. Focus mostly on identifying positive behaviors in which they honored God or reflected Christian love during the day. When applicable, you can also invite them to talk about areas in which they need to improve their behavior, but do so only in a positive, hopeful light so that your children don't begin to dread your bedtime conversations. Emphasize that God loves them unconditionally, and you do too! For example, if a child recalls that he needs to work on sharing toys, you might say, "You're right. You can make God very happy and show his love by sharing. And guess what! God can help you share! God is very proud of you for trying to become a better sharer, and so am I!"

zero in with prayer

If you've spent any time practicing the disciplines already outlined in the first few chapters of this book, then you've certainly heard from God about at least one area of your life in which he wants you to grow and change. True listening to God and openness to his Word inevitably (and quickly) leads us to identify ways in which we can better honor God and imitate Jesus in our daily living. One of the most important ways to effect life change (and to avoid the Ben Franklin syndrome) is to zero in on your need for God's help through prayer. At the conclusion of his powerful little book *Humility—The Beauty of Holiness*, Andrew Murray challenged readers to spend a month intensely focusing on humility in prayer. He wrote, "Be always inwardly longing, and earnestly praying this one prayer to God: 'That of His great goodness He would make known to you, and take from your heart, every kind and form and degree of Pride . . . and that He would awaken in you the deepest depth and truth of that Humility, which can make you capable of His light and Holy Spirit.'"[3] Murray sug-

[I]t may be said that every act of [the Christian's] life is or can be as truly sacred as prayer or baptism or the Lord's Supper. . . . That we see this truth is not enough. . . . We must practice living to the glory of God, actually and determinedly.

—A. W. Tozer

79

gested that those who zealously pray in this manner for a sustained period of time will experience changes in their heart.

You can practice this same life-change tool by praying about a specific area of your life in which God is prompting you to change. Simply compose a brief written prayer that focuses on the area in which God is convicting you, then commit to pray it often and regularly for a set period of time. You'll be amazed at how much this pointed attention to prayer will remind you of your reliance on the Holy Spirit's power and will make you attentive to the daily situations in which you can enact that change.

form an action plan

Beyond self-examination and prayer, we must commit to do something about the areas in which we need change. As God reveals to you an area in which you need to grow, formulate a plan of attack. How will you put effort toward overcoming that sin or fostering that virtue with the help of the Holy Spirit? How will you identify and resist temptations? Come up with one to three specific steps you'll take to grow. Here are some examples:

- Write down your life-change goal on an index card and post it in an area where you will see it often.

- Do something proactive related to your area of life change, such as doing hard work to combat laziness, intentionally playing with your child to overcome feelings of irritation, or sending an encouraging note to someone with whom you're annoyed.

- Confess your struggle to a Christian friend and request accountability and prayer support.

- Memorize a Bible verse related to your area of life change and recite it several times throughout the day.

- Talk to a mentor or older Christian about the issue, asking for advice and guidance.

- Read a Christian book on the area you're focusing on and journal your thoughts.

Once you've identified at least one specific step, take it! Move beyond goal setting to action.

keep seeking

In spite of the pressure we put on ourselves, we don't have to live up to our culture's unrealistic expectation that we should "have it all together." We don't have to put forth a false image in which we always look perfect, mother perfectly, perform perfectly at work, keep a perfect house, and live a perfect Christian life. While performing well in all areas may be our goal, there is no harm in admitting that we haven't yet reached it. Each of us is a work in progress. By openly acknowledging this truth before our family and friends, we defy the cultural lie that says we can only feel good about ourselves if everyone else thinks we've got our act together. We instead live openly and honestly with our husband, children, and our friends, admitting that there are areas in which we are trying to grow.

When we willingly acknowledge to others that, with God's help, we are trying to overcome sin or grow in specific areas, we glorify God! We demonstrate that we are seeking to please God and that we are relying on God to empower us to change. Furthermore, by openly identifying the areas we're working on, we automatically enlist the help of family members and friends. One mom experienced this reality in a funny—and humbling—way: "At the end of a rough day, I was putting my three-year-old daughter to bed and apologized for having been grouchy that day. She said it was OK and gave me a hug. The next morning at breakfast, she prayed for each family member, and then as a side thought, asked God to 'help Mommy not be so grouchy today. Amen' I didn't know whether to be stunned or be humbled!"

It probably didn't feel good to have her faults pointed out in prayer by her daughter, but the reminder helped that mom focus even more wholeheartedly on her effort to exhibit cheerful patience. And it clearly helped her daughter learn that we can and should turn to God for help in becoming more Christlike. This type of raw living in front of your kids will help them discover how to live authentically as they come to sense the reality of God's grace and your reliance on it. As another mom put it, "I think my daughter learns most in the moments when I am most real with her. When I realize I am being impatient, I tell her, 'I am feeling very impatient right now' and she says, 'Please be patient, Mommy.' It is almost like having an additional conscience."

As both moms pointed out, a key part of living as a work in progress is being willing to recognize and apologize for times we've

God draws us—you and me—up to his light. Our progress isn't always easy. We encounter sticks or stones or mountain ranges in this quest. Our learning curve is steep. We keep slipping back, making side trips. But once we have heard the divine summons nothing else will seem adequate around which to structure our lives.

—Luci Shaw

messed up. When appropriate, we can also share with our children what we're doing to change by saying something like "I'm sorry I got so angry today. I'm trying to do a better job dealing with my feelings, and I'm asking God to help me. I'm doing my best to show God I love him by trying to live the way he wants me to."

Making the radical choice to be a continual seeker after life change is challenging because it runs contrary to our perfectionist tendencies and the cultural definition of success for women. Yet at the same time, it is incredibly freeing. We can live as we really are—and those around are able to see the power of God at work as he carries on to completion the good work he has begun in us.

a life of contradictions

In this life, we will always battle sin, faults, and failings. Yet as we choose to look deeply into the truth about our daily living, we are equipped to live as doers of God's Word and his promptings in our lives. And as we persevere in our efforts to examine our living and commit to life change, we will be blessed in our doing. Change won't be easy, but we can take heart in the knowledge that Jesus will not fail us. Through his salvation, grace, and forgiveness, we can live new lives.

As you consider how the discipline of life change can become a more consistent part of your life, take heart from the words of the Apostle Paul, here rendered by Eugene Peterson in *The Message:*

If I know the law but still can't keep it, and if the power of sin within me keeps sabotaging my best intentions, I obviously need help! I realize that I don't have what it takes. I can will it, but I can't do it. I decide to do good, but I don't really do it; I decide not to do bad, but then I do it anyway. My decisions, such as they are, don't result in actions. Something has gone wrong deep within me and gets the better of me every time. . . . I've tried everything and nothing helps. I'm at the end of my rope. Is there no one who can do anything for me? Isn't that the real question?

The answer, thank God, is that Jesus Christ can and does. He acted to set things right in this life of contradictions where I want to serve God with all my heart and mind, but am pulled by the influence of sin to do something totally different.

With the arrival of Jesus, the Messiah, that fateful dilemma is resolved. Those who enter into Christ's being-here-for-us no longer have to live under a continuous, low-lying black cloud. A new power is in operation. The Spirit of life in Christ, like a strong wind, has magnificently cleared the air, freeing you from a fated lifetime of brutal tyranny at the hands of sin and death. (Rom. 7:17–20, 24–25; 8:1–2)

talk about it

Discuss these questions with a friend or a small group of other moms.

1. Have you ever had an embarrassing experience like the one described at the start of this chapter? What happened?

2. How would you describe the relationship between *doing* (also called *good works*) and *faith*?

3. When have you recently felt compelled to apply a scriptural truth or a prompting from God to your life? Were you able to put that conviction into action? Why or why not?

4. How is the Holy Spirit currently prompting you to grow or change? Share one specific area.

5. Which of the approaches to life change described in this chapter do you feel compelled to try out or make a habit? Why?

84

try it

Here are ten ideas you can try.

1. Read these Scripture passages about life change: John 15:1–8; Romans 7:4–6, 12:1–2; Galatians 5:22–24; Ephesians 2:8–10; Philippians 1:6; and James 1:21–25. How well are they reflected in your life? In what ways do you desire to grow in this discipline? Journal your thoughts.

2. Commit to practice examen daily for a week. Decide ahead of time what your approach will be and when you'll do it. For example, you could commit to five minutes of prayerful review while lying in bed each night, or you could determine to spend twenty minutes journaling your responses to John Wesley's questions right after you tuck the kids in at night.

3. If you feel overwhelmed because there are many areas in your life in which you know you need to grow and change, decide to focus just on one for now. Write down the specific area you'll focus on and spell out a realistic growth goal based on God's promptings.

4. Using Ignatius's contemplative reading approach (see page 77), explore the story of Zacchaeus in Luke 19:1–10. Afterward, spend time comparing your response to Zacchaeus's. Why was

he so eager to make concrete changes to his life? How can you foster that attitude in your own life?

5. Apologize to your child or husband for something you've done wrong. Ask their forgiveness and tell them that you're striving to grow in that area with God's help.

6. Write a short prayer that zeros in on an area of life change. Commit to pray it at least once daily during the upcoming week.

7. Memorize Psalm 139:23–24 and pray it several times a day. Then listen to God's leading. He may point something out to you when you're least expecting it!

8. Tell a Christian friend about an area in your life in which you are trying to grow. Ask for prayer and accountability.

9. Has God been prompting you to respond to him by taking a specific action? If so, commit to do it. Write your commitment here.

_____

_____

_____

_____

_____

_____

_____

_____

_____

_____

10. Meditate on Romans 7:17–8:2 from *The Message* or from a traditional translation, focusing on what 8:1–2 means in your own life.

6

service

C heck out this typical day in the life of Tracy, a mother of two-year-old twin boys who is also five months pregnant with baby number three.

Our day starts at 6:00 a.m., and Ethan and Carl want breakfast right away. I try to be awake enough to make sure the right boy gets the red bib and the other one gets the blue, or a major meltdown occurs. Once the boys decide whether they want peanut butter, jelly, or honey on their toast and whether they want their cereal on their tray or in a bowl with milk, I usually have a few minutes to wolf down my toast before they begin round two.

On most mornings breakfast is followed by playtime, though the concept of sharing is not well understood by the twins; like most toddlers, they seem to think that if they have played with a toy at any point in time it belongs solely to them. When one boy "steals" a toy from another, a scratching-wrestling fight ensues. When they're not fighting with each other, they're usually getting into trouble as a team. Yesterday they simultaneously took their diapers off, emptied them on the floor, and ran around screeching.

Things happen fast around here. Often I'll be talking to one boy and look over my shoulder to see crayon scribbles on the fridge or cereal dumped on the floor. Today I was picking up clothes off the floor and turned around to see them using a cardboard wrapping paper roll as a battering ram on the TV. They thought it was hilarious. I always wondered how kids could get away with such crazy things. I figured their parents were just lazy or inattentive. Now I know that kids are stinkin' *fast*. They pull these stunts right before your eyes!

If I have to run errands, I try to get the boys all ready and gather all the necessary things long before we need to leave because it takes so long to get them ready. After going through the car-seat Olympics with one twin, I head back into the house to grab the other. It's not surprising to find a pile of coat, shoes, pants, and diaper on the floor and a naked toddler running around the living room squealing.

After running errands, it's back home for lunch. Then we change diapers, brush teeth, and read a story or two before naptime. The boys have mastered the technique of asking for "one more," and if I go for that they always ask for a third. At least they're learning to count!

Once they're in bed for their nap, I usually attack some chore like paying bills, catching up on e-mail, or making a few phone calls. Just occasionally I take a plain old nap. Then, like clockwork, Carl wakes up and begins shouting one of his two favorite words: *Cheese!* and *Snack!*

Soon after their nap, we sit down for dinner number one because the boys are ready to eat long before their dad gets home. When my husband arrives, we try to eat dinner number two together while managing the kids. When we finally put them to bed at night, I'm exhausted. I usually hit the sack early just to get enough energy for the next day . . . when it starts all over again.

Does anything in that daily routine sound familiar? You may not have your hands as full as Tracy does—or a typical day in your life may even be more chaotic. If anything, mothers with small children are *busy!* How on earth could someone whose life looks like this have any time or energy left over to devote to serving others? Is it even possible?

love in action

For a mom like Tracy—and for you—service is likely a spiritual discipline you're already practicing every day, even if you don't realize it. Mother Teresa defined service as "love in action."[1] And she wasn't talking merely about mere feelings of affection. *Agape* is the Greek word used in the New Testament to describe divine love: the generous, ultimate love God has for all of humanity. It is this divine love that we are urged to show to both our friends (Mark 12:28–31) and enemies (Matt. 5:43–48). In fact, the word *charity*, which people often use synonymously with *service*, actually comes from the Latin version of *agape*: *caritas*. Practicing the discipline of service means taking concrete action to demonstrate God's love to another person.

The discipline of service was a top priority for Jesus, who taught, "Whoever wants to become great among you must be your servant" (Matt. 20:26) and demonstrated the point during his last night of fellowship with the disciples before his arrest and crucifixion. At the start of the Last Supper, Jesus literally became a servant when he knelt down to wash the disciples' feet. This thankless (and probably smelly!) task was routinely done by household servants. Afterward, Jesus asked the disciples,

"Do you understand what I have done for you? . . . You call me 'Teacher' and 'Lord,' and rightly so, for that is what I am. Now that I, your Lord and Teacher, have washed your feet, you also should wash one another's feet. *I have set you an example that you should do as I have done for you.*" (John 13:12–15, emphasis added)

89

You and I are Jesus' disciples today, and we, too, are called to follow his example by serving others, even when those tasks are lowly, boring, routine, mundane, exhausting, taxing, or thankless. Sometimes serving means meeting physical needs through practical means such as providing food, shelter, or help to the poor or sick. At other times this means addressing emotional and spiritual needs through acts of kindness, mercy, and friendship.

> The real test of the saint is not preaching the gospel, but washing disciples' feet, that is, doing the things that do not count in the actual estimate of men but count everything in the estimate of God.
>
> —Oswald Chambers

rethinking daily drudgery

Regardless of the *means* of service, it is our *motivation* for serving others that makes our action a meaningful spiritual discipline. We do not serve because we should, because we have to, or in order to generate good feelings about "making a difference." We serve because our example, Jesus "made himself nothing, taking the form of a servant" (Phil. 2:7 ESV) in order to demonstrate his deep love for humankind. We serve others—whether it be the poor, a neighbor, a shut-in, or our families—because we choose to love others in the same lavish way in which God loves us. Ultimately, we serve others as an act of worship toward God. Eugene Peterson remarked that "The service we offer to God (in worship) is extended into specific acts that serve others. We learn a relationship—an attitude toward life, a stance—of servitude before God, and then we are available to be of use to others in acts of service."[2] As we develop this attitude toward life that is focused on serving God, we inevitably discover that our daily routines are already jam-packed with chances to serve others.

Though my friend Tracy doesn't have many opportunities during this season of her life to participate in organized service projects, such as volunteering at a soup kitchen, for her—and for you—each day is a portrait of service. Responsibilities at home can be meaningful acts of service: feeding children, wiping noses, doing laundry, mowing the lawn. Likewise, tasks at the office can be spiritual acts of service when undertaken with the motive of demonstrating divine love. Things like working with excellence in order to contribute to the good of others, doing extra work on a task in order to benefit a colleague or sending an encouraging e-mail to a team member can be acts of service. Whether you're a working mom or a stay-at-home mom, your daily drudgery can be transformed into meaningful service to God and others; it's simply a matter of taking on a Romans 12:1 (MSG) mind-set: "So here's what I want you to do, God helping you: Take your everyday, ordinary life—your sleeping, eating, going-to-work, and walking-around life—and place it before God as an offering."

recognizing kid-style service

Until your little kids reach a behavioral maturity level, it isn't wise to take them along on service projects that are geared for adults, such as working at a homeless shelter or helping to build a house with Habitat for Humanity. If your kids are too young, you'll spend most of your time trying to keep them safe or out of trouble, and they'll distract you and others from the purpose of the project. But even while they are young, there are lots of meaningful things kids can do to show God's love to others.

Putting the Picture Pile to Good Use. I'm inspired by the amazingly simple and meaningful way my friend Rachel gets her kids involved in serving others. It all began when Rachel and her daughters went to visit her elderly great-aunt and took along some crayon pictures for her. Later, Rachel got to thinking. She realized that her three-year-old daughter did lots of drawing and painting. Rachel had so many pictures and crafts items lying around the house that she didn't have room for them all. That's when it dawned on her. Why not start giving pictures and crafts as gifts to nursing home residents? "My daughter got very excited about the idea," Rachel related. "Now when we make visits to the nursing home, she brings her drawings and hands them out to everyone she sees! Now I don't get busted by my daughter pitifully asking, 'Mommy, why did you throw away my picture?' (Ouch!) When our pile at home gets too high, we know it is time to make another trip to the nursing home."

This meaningful ray of sunshine for nursing home residents is simple and fun for Rachel's young daughter; and it's something your kids could do, too, by visiting either a nursing home or the elderly or shut-ins in your neighborhood. Do you have a growing stack of drawings, coloring book pages, and crafts from home, church, or preschool? Put them to good use!

Serving Siblings. If you have more than one child, you've got a ready-made opportunity to teach your older kids to serve by giving them opportunities to help, care for, or comfort their younger siblings. Be careful of going overboard with this idea, in which case your older child may begin viewing his or her younger siblings as annoyances. But in small doses, this practice can give kids the experience of serving God by serving others.

For example, you could ask an older child to fetch a diaper for you as you care for an infant, or you could prompt the older child to offer a hug and some encouraging words to a younger brother or sister with a skinned knee or stubbed toe. Make sure to reinforce for your child the idea that he or she is worshiping God by serving and caring for someone else. You might say saying something like "Thanks so much for showing Jesus' love to your little sister!"

Prettying Up the Park. Make it a habit to bring a trash bag along each time you and your kids make a visit to a local

> You can keep kids' hands clean by having them wear plastic sandwich bags as "mittens" when they pick up trash.

park or playground. After the kids play, invite them to join you in spending a few minutes cleaning up pieces of trash littering the park. This is something you could do even with a one-year-old! Sure, he may pick up just one piece of trash (with your help), but it's a good way to begin a great habit. Let your kids know you're really proud of them for serving God by cleaning up his creation and by serving the other kids who will use the park by making it nice and clean.

Doing Chores with a Purpose. Just as you can focus the tasks of your daily routine on service by maintaining a proper motivation, you can help your kids make the connection between service and household chores. If your kids are too little to have daily or weekly chores, you can still invite them to help you out once in awhile. About the time he turned two, my son, Davis, suddenly thought it was a blast to "sweep" the kitchen (that is, to push dirt from one spot to another with a kid-sized broom) and "clean" the tub (meaning to rub it with a Kleenex tissue). Though enlisting the "help" of little ones may actually make the job more work, it encourages them to serve the rest of the family. As they work, you can remind them, "You're doing a great job showing Jesus' love by helping our family have a clean house!"

93

putting it into action: mom-friendly ideas

Along with those simple principles for enabling kids to serve others, here are some suggestions for doable, practical ways you can serve those in need in the midst of your busy-mom lifestyle.

go postal

You can show love toward people who are hurting and lonely without leaving your house by "going postal!" All you have to do is invest a little money in purchasing fifty-two blank cards and fifty-two stamps. Determine to send one encouraging note each week to someone who is lonely, hurting, distressed, confused, or spiritually hungry. Throughout the week, spend time praying and listening to God about whom he may want you to serve with words of hope and encouragement. God *will* put someone on your mind! You might also call your church office to find out who is having surgery, dealing with a loss or illness, pregnant, about to

> We can cure physical diseases with medicine, but the only cure for loneliness, despair, and hopelessness is love. There are many in the world who are dying for a piece of bread but there are many more dying for a little love. . . . There's a hunger for love, as there is a hunger for God.
>
> —Mother Teresa

be married, or serving on the mission field and could use a bit of encouragement. It will take only ten or fifteen minutes to write a meaningful note, address it, and put it in the mail, but God will magnify your efforts in mighty ways by touching the heart of the card's recipient!

coordinate others' efforts

Though your responsibilities with your kids may prevent you from participating directly in church-sponsored service projects, you can still contribute. Often the most important part of producing a service project is the work done behind the scenes—date setting, coordinating volunteers, arranging for transportation, and generating publicity. Consider taking on some of the administrative work that's required to make a service project happen. One mom I know helps facilitate her church's free English classes for recent immigrants by coordinating the schedules of the volunteer teachers and reminding them when they're scheduled to work via phone or e-mail. It's not the hands-on involvement she'd like to have; but without her willingness to serve in this way, the program wouldn't run smoothly. Another mom felt God prompting her to coordinate a mini clothing drive among the members of her adult Sunday School class to benefit the homeless. All she had to do was set a date for collecting clothing, invite people to bring items to the church, ask a volunteer to load the items into her minivan, and then drop them off at the downtown mission. The class responded generously, and the spur-of-the-moment service project went off without a hitch.

How about you? Are there ways you could get involved in making service projects happen, even if you're not able to participate in the actual event? Pray about ways you can get involved from home by taking on some administrative chores. Then see where God leads you.

minister to moms in need

Kids usually can't go along on "grown-up" service projects, but you can serve together by ministering to other moms and their kids. For example, if there's a local shelter for homeless or battered women and children in your area, you might see if there are ways you could get involved there. You might be able to bring your own kids along while you volunteer for simple tasks such as leading a weekly story time for the young children at the shelter or directing a craft activity. Usually, family shelters also need people to volunteer for tutoring children, babysitting kids while their moms look for a job, or helping with cooking.

Another group of moms in need are women who've just gone through a crisis pregnancy. Christian crisis pregnancy centers and teen mothers' groups are often looking for women who will be mentor moms to new mothers who are learning the ropes of motherhood. This can be a high level of commitment, or it could be as simple as inviting a new mom and her child to come over for a play date at your house for an hour every week or two. You will meet real needs by lending a listening ear, offering parenting advice (when asked), and supplying the new mom with lots of encouragement and prayer.

If you hear about a mom in your neighborhood or from your church family who is facing a hard time—such as depression, a family loss, stress and exhaustion, illness, marriage troubles, or financial woes—you can give her some space to breathe and sort things out by offering a few hours of free babysitting.

watch for spontaneous service opportunities

Mother Teresa considered it an essential ingredient of service to be willing "to be inspired by the Holy Spirit to act when called."[3] Along with the purposeful practices of service already discussed, the Holy Spirit often presents spontaneous opportunities to serve those in need—we simply need to keep our eyes open for the opportunities and our hearts attentive to hear the Holy Spirit's call.

One day my kids and I were stopped at an intersection on our way home from the zoo and we saw a homeless man standing on a downtown corner. He was holding a sign that read "Hungry. Need help." I quickly glanced in my purse and saw that there wasn't any spare change, but something else caught my eye: the granola bar my son hadn't eaten at the zoo. It was still unopened! I rolled down the window and handed it to the man. And that was that—nothing fancy, no warm fuzzies, just a simple exchange. As I drove on, I wondered, *What if I were always prepared with something like that to give to a person in need? Would it be so hard to keep a few granola bars and bottles of water in the van?* We now make it a habit to bring some ready-response supplies with us when we drive downtown, just in case God sends someone hungry our way.

What about you? What are some spontaneous opportunities to serve others that God has sent your way? As you dedicate your everyday, ordinary life to God with a willingness to show his divine love to others through service, he will give you opportunities to do just that. It may be something as simple as holding the door open for an elderly person at the grocery store, picking up a piece of trash on a neighbor's lawn, or calling a lonely friend whom God has placed on your heart. Ask God how he wants you to be ready, and then be prepared to respond to his call.

embracing the privilege

Whether you're coordinating the administrative details that enable others to do hands-on service or just trying to make it through a day of refereeing fights between your kids, changing diapers, and attempting to run errands, remember that as you focus your heart on following Christ's example of love, your actions will have eternal significance! In fact, doing the most mundane tasks of motherhood can far surpass the loveliest praise song as an act of worship when we are motivated by genuine love. So during those crazy days like the one Tracy described at the outset of this chapter, echo in your heart the sentiment of Mother Teresa: "It is a privilege for us to serve, and it's a real, wholehearted service that we try to give."[4]

talk about it

Discuss these questions with a friend or a small group of other moms.

1. Think through a typical day in your life. What are some of the things you do, big or small, in order to meet the needs of others?

2. What do you think about Mother Teresa's definition of service? How would you define service in your own words?

3. Why was serving others such an important focus of Jesus' teachings? How does Jesus' example of service inspire you? convict you?

4. What are your dreams for your children when it comes to serving others? What do you want them to experience, learn, and understand about serving those in need?

5. Which idea for integrating the discipline of service into your life stands out to you most? Why?

try it

Here are ten ideas you can try.

1. Read these Scripture passages about service: Matthew 20:20–28, John 13:1–17, Romans 12:1, Galatians 5:13–14, Ephesians 6:7, and Philippians 2:1–11. How do you want your mind-set about service to change in light of what the Bible teaches? Journal your thoughts.

2. Remind yourself to view your routine tasks as opportunities to lovingly serve others by frequently reciting this paraphrase of Mother Teresa's teaching: "It is a privilege for me to serve, and it is a real, wholehearted service that I will try to give."

3. Decide on one realistic commitment you can make to help coordinate a service project that other adults in your church can participate in. Even though you'll miss out on some of the hands-on work, your administrative efforts will be putting love into action!

4. Identify one way you can use your child's crafts to serve the emotional needs of someone who is hurting or lonely, such as a shut-in, nursing home resident, or sick member of your church family. Talk to your child about this opportunity to show Jesus' love. Then deliver the pictures and crafts together.

5. Reflect on the past week or two and identify occasions when you missed the chance to serve others. Prayerfully come up with one practical step you can take, such as carrying spare change or snacks for the poor, so that you will be ready to respond to spontaneous needs.

6. Pop in a favorite CD of worship music the next time you set about cleaning or some other household drudgery. Sing along

while you work, reminding yourself that your service to your family is also an act of worship toward God.

7. Ask God to show you how you and your kids can minister to a mother in need. Contact your church office, a crisis pregnancy center, or a women and children's shelter to identify a person or area of need you can respond to.

8. Spend a week focusing on helping your children learn the value of service by implementing one kid-sized act of service each day, such as sweeping the kitchen together, picking up trash, washing the car, helping to cook a meal, or sorting laundry. Each time, praise your children heartily for showing God's love by meeting the needs of others.

9. Meditate on the words of Jesus in Matthew 20:26.

10. Do some "postal" service by sending an anonymous note of encouragement to someone who is hurting.

99

7

evangelism
and hospitality

I was simultaneously excited and nervous when a non-Christian acquaintance I'd met in our neighborhood came over because she wanted to talk about spiritual issues—what a great opportunity to share my faith! As we sat at the dining room table, drinking coffee and beginning with small talk, my son was contentedly playing with Legos nearby. But as our conversation moved to some of my new friend's spiritual questions, I noticed a strange, creeped-out expression on her face. Then she began giggling.

What's so funny? I wondered. *Did I say something stupid?* Soon I realized the cause of my friend's laughter: My son had crawled under the table and was rubbing her calves and feet. He was absolutely fascinated with the texture of her nylons!

"Um, sorry about that," I said, embarrassed, as I settled my son down with some crayons and other craft supplies in the adjacent kitchen. My friend and I resumed our conversation, and soon we were able to dive back into spiritual subjects. My little guy appeared to be playing quietly, and all was well. But after awhile, something registered in my brain. *He's being too quiet*, I thought. *He's up to something.*

I excused myself from the conversation and found my son with his children's scissors in hand and a chunk of hair on the floor. "Mommy, look!" he said proudly. "That's my hair!" *Ugh. This is pointless!*

I realized I'd have to adjourn the conversation with my neighbor and hoped we could pick it up another time. No matter that I was trying to do something with an eternal impact, it was unrealistic to expect my young son to be able to play by himself and simply hope he didn't get into trouble.

So that was that. Unfortunately, my guest and I never got around to any of the truths about Christ I really wanted to share that day. I realized that the thing she'd probably remember most from our meeting was the shock of feeling my son under the table cuddling with her ankles! And to top it off, the little bruiser now had girlish bangs!

So much for evangelism.

101

evangelism plain and simple

Evangelism is often just plain scary. It makes us fear that our friends may think we're weird, judgmental, or pushy, or that we'll be asked questions we can't answer. We're intimidated by the negative impressions our friends have of Christianity, and we're nervous that we won't know what to say or, worse, that we'll say exactly the wrong things. So it can be tempting to make the inconvenience (or seeming impossibility) of trying to witness

According to The Barna Group, only 34 percent of adults feel that they have a personal responsibility to talk to others about their religious beliefs.

while caring for children a comfy excuse for not evangelizing. But there is no season in life, no matter how busy and stressful, in which we can take time out from evangelizing. Jesus' commission, "you will be my witnesses" (Acts 1:8), applies to us as busy moms just as much as it applied to Jesus' first disciples.

At its core, practicing the discipline of evangelism is a simple matter: Motivated by God's love, we honestly and openly speak with others about our interactions with Jesus. The woman at the well in John 4:1–42 is a compelling example of what evangelism looks like in its most raw form. She wasn't a longtime disciple of Jesus; in fact, she'd only had one brief conversation with him. But look at her immediate response to that interaction: "Then, leaving her water jar, the woman went back to the town and said to the people, 'Come, see a man who told me everything I ever did. Could this be the Christ?'" (John 4:28–29). Her message was simple and to the point. She merely shared from her heart about her amazing encounter with Jesus. Then she encouraged others to "come, see" Jesus for themselves. John went on to record that many of the Samaritans from that town believed in Jesus as a result of this woman's message (John 4:39). Like her, you can share openly about your relationship with Jesus and invite others to meet him too. Though evangelism certainly will look different now than in other stages of life (when you actually *can* have a quiet conversation over coffee), we must still do what we can.

from stranger danger to neighbor love

When it comes to the discipline of hospitality, let's toss out the idea of keeping a perfectly clean home and serving a flawlessly prepared meal to invited dinner guests—that isn't what hospitality is truly about. The New Testament word for hospitality is *philoxenia,* and its meaning is simple: to demonstrate brother love (*phileo*) to strangers (*xenia*). Right off the bat, this definition is frightening. Don't we teach our children that all-important mantra "Don't talk to strangers"? Shouldn't we model the principle of stranger danger to our kids?

Though we certainly should do our best to keep our kids safe and make wise decisions, we must not allow a stranger-danger mind-set poison our spiritual perspective. When it comes to hospitality—showing love to strangers—we must take seriously Jesus' response to a group of people at the final judgment:

> [O]ffering hospitality is a moral imperative. . . . This expectation is not based on any special immunity to the dangers unknown people might present—far from it. Rather, it emerges from knowing the hospitality God has shown us.
>
> —Ana Maria Piñeda

103

"I was hungry and you gave me no food, I was thirsty and you gave me no drink, *I was a stranger and you did not welcome me*, naked and you did not clothe me, sick and in prison and you did not visit me." Then they also will answer, saying, "Lord, when did we see you hungry or thirsty or *a stranger* or naked or sick or in prison, and did not minister to you?" Then he will answer them, saying, "Truly, I say to you, *as you did not do it to one of the least of these, you did not do it to me*." (Matt. 25:42–45 ESV, emphasis added)

None of us wants to reflect on our lives and realize that we never spoke with, showed love to, or ministered to strangers!

One of Jesus' most memorable parables is about hospitality, and it doesn't take place in a June Cleaver–like home but along the side of a dusty road. In the story of the Good Samaritan (Luke

10:25–37), two different religious leaders walk right by a man who's lying on the side of the road, severely beaten, stripped of his clothes, robbed, and left for dead. Then a Samaritan walks by and responds with love, caring for the man's wounds, taking him to an inn, and providing money to meet the man's other needs. The Samaritan chooses to treat the stranger as a neighbor, and, as Jesus points out, then loves this neighbor as himself. The story is even more impressive when you know that in those days it was the Samaritan who would have been considered an outsider. When we practice hospitality, we choose to love like the Samaritan man did.

When we practice evangelism and hospitality, we

- View all people as neighbors, whom we are to love. We see them with compassion and grace as people treasured by God.

- Seek to share the message and love of Jesus with all people because of our God-inspired love for them.

- Rely on the Holy Spirit to lead us, equip us with the right words, and enable us to overcome our fears.

- Offer willingly our homes, talents, time, and abilities to be used by God and directed for his purposes.

- Determine to treat others as if they were Jesus in disguise (Matt. 25:37–40).

- Leave the results of our actions in God's hands and relinquish a sense of personal responsibility for our "success" or "failure."

God's amazing love is the foundation for the twin disciplines of evangelism and hospitality. Motivated by this love, we *go out* to reach others with the message of Christ (evangelism); and because of this love, we *invite in* others to care for them with the grace of Christ (hospitality). This cycle of going out and inviting in is what some have called lifestyle evangelism, pairing our words about Christ with caring actions that demonstrate the gospel we preach.

putting it into action: mom-friendly ideas

At this point you may be wishing you had skipped this chapter. Evangelism and hospitality can certainly be . . . uncomfortable. Add to this the reality that your kids disrupt or interrupt most of your efforts at both practices, and these disciplines begin to seem impossible. But they're not! There are several ways busy moms can effectively practice evangelism and hospitality—it just takes a little creativity, a sense of adventure, and a willingness to step out of your comfort zone.

start with your neighborhood

When it comes to loving your neighbor as yourself, the best place to start out is in your own neighborhood. God has surrounded you with neighbors—next door, down the street, around the block, in the apartment upstairs. You and your children can reach out to them, get to know them, and show them about Jesus through your loving actions and words. One easy way to begin is by identifying any neighbors who have kids your children's age—you may naturally meet them at the neighborhood playground or on a walk. Take the initiative to start a conversation: Parents love to talk about their kids! Then make sure to connect personally by finding out about the neighbor's job and spouse, and by exchanging names. (If you don't have a good memory, write down your new friends' names as soon as you get home.)

Two friends of mine have made it a habit to creatively reach out to others (along with their kids) during holiday seasons. One friend, Jen, employed her son, Miah, to help her make and decorate

Christmas cookies. Then they walked down their street together, pulling a red wagon full of cookie bags. (She lives in California—you might need to modify this idea if you live in the frigid Midwest like I do!) Each bag had a card her son colored that wished the recipient a merry Christmas and included my friend's name and the location of her house. This simple act opened many doors of conversation as neighbors stopped by to say thank you to Miah for the holiday gift.

My second outreach-oriented friend, Jim, created a map of his immediate neighborhood and took it along as he and his kids went trick-or-treating on Halloween. He invited the neighbors he met to share their name, phone number, and the names of their kids so he could create a neighborhood directory. Jim promised to make copies and distribute them to everyone who participated. The relationship building that resulted from this one simple action was phenomenal!

Whether your outreach idea uses holidays or simple acts like inviting another mom to go on exercise walks around the neighborhood or committing to always talk to other parents at the playground, you can bloom right where God has planted you.

target other moms

Sometimes mothering can be a lonely task. As a result of caring for children, you have few opportunities to pursue your own interests and to build friendships with other adults. If you think you're lonely, imagine what's going on in the hearts of busy moms who don't have the love of God in their lives. The feelings of isolation that sometimes accompany motherhood are magnified for women who don't have a strong spiritual foundation based on their relationship with God. In addition to reaching out to those who happen to live near you, with a little innovation you can take advantage of opportunities to meet other moms who may be hurting or who need to know about God's love.

If you're a working mom, one easy way to begin building relationships with other moms is to go on a cubicle scout in your office. During a break, take a walk around your workplace and look for pictures of children on women's desks. Then start a conversation about the kids. If your kids attend daycare or preschool, be intentional about arriving a few minutes before pickup time in order to start conversations (even if they're brief) with other parents. Stay-at-home moms can meet new friends by taking advantage of community activities. One friend of mine has built a great relationship with a non-Christian mom that began in the bleachers of the local swimming pool during her daughter's swimming lessons. One way I've been able to meet other moms is by attending the free story time at our local library. Lots of opportunities like this exist— you just need to be on the lookout!

107

share meals

You don't have to be a stellar housekeeper or gourmet cook to use your home to minister to others in life-impacting ways—you just have to be willing to offer your space, time, and possessions to God and invite him to use them for his purposes. Opening up your home to others is a countercultural idea nowadays, but spending time with another person in a home (or backyard, or even garage!) can be a catalyst for meaningful relationship growth. As we share our space, we implicitly begin to share more of our real lives.

Remember my friend Jim who created a neighborhood directory on Halloween night? Once the map with accompanying names was developed, the entire family went around the block together delivering the directories and inviting neighbors to pop in for soup at their house on an upcoming evening. Soon this became a monthly tradition. Now on the last Friday of each month, neighbors come over (some bearing food to share) for a time of talking, games, and playtime for the little kids. As a result of this relationship building, my friends have been able to initiate several spiritual conversations about their relationship with Jesus.

If a once-a-month block party at your house sounds overwhelming, start with just one family and invite them over for dinner. If children are coming, too, do a kid-friendly meal like assembling simple pizzas and baking them together or concocting ice cream sundaes. You can also put wheels to your hospitality by taking meals (or a batch of cookies or banana bread) on the road, dropping them off at the home of a friend or neighbor who has had a new baby, is battling an illness, or has experienced a significant loss. And if cooking a meal just isn't your thing, you can still use your home to minister to others by inviting a mom and her kids over for a play date and a Coke.

keep a guest room

Perhaps the most radical way to practice hospitality is to have a designated guest room in your house and be willing to let others use it. I'm not talking only about family members who've popped in for a visit—I mean straight-up, Good-Samaritan-style caring for a guest. One mom I know, Sara, puts her guestroom to work by inviting visiting missionaries stay in her home for a night or two. She sees it as a meaningful way to support global missions and always does her best to make the experience a blessing by giving attention to small details like putting chocolates on the pillows and shower gel in the bathroom.

My friend Katie provided a stunning example of hospitality when she and her husband invited an exchange student—a Muslim teenage boy—to live in their home for a year. At that time Katie not only was raising a two-year-old but also was pregnant. Her family's experience with their exchange student brought lots of challenges, such as the time when Katie was walking home with her daughter from the neighborhood pool and heard obscenity-laden rap music blasting all over the neighborhood—from her home stereo! Despite its challenges, this act of outreach and kindness enabled Katie to demonstrate service and kindness while sharing an authentic, Christ-focused lifestyle with someone who had never before met a Christian.

Many types of people are in great need of hospitality. One usually overlooked group of people is international college students. Imagine how meaningful it would be to someone from another country to be invited to stay with an American family during Christmas break! This type of outreach, especially over holidays, provides ample opportunities to share the "why" behind family traditions. Others who may need a soft place to land are those who've been displaced by storms or house fires, pregnant teenagers facing troubles at home, or women escaping domestic violence. Opportunities like these may be rare, but don't be surprised if God asks you to make your guestroom into a space for true ministry as you keep your heart open to his leading.

109

share the good news

Sharing our faith through actions often seems easier than using words to tell others about spiritual things—especially when our efforts to talk are constantly interrupted by child-rearing demands. Yet there are ways we busy moms can verbally share our faith, even in little snippets. When life gets too hectic for sustained conversation, it's critical to keep in mind that the weight of "success" in evangelism is not on our shoulders. In 1 Corinthians 3:6, Paul pointed this out about the process of converting nonbelievers: "I planted the seed, Apollos watered it, but God made it grow." Sometimes God's purpose for our spiritual conversations may be only to plant a seed; at other times we may be watering a person's growing interest in Jesus; and sometimes we are blessed to be the harvesters who lead others into a faith relationship with Jesus after God has cultivated their hearts.

When we have opportunities to talk with another person about spiritual things, whether it's during a break at work or on a playground bench, we can often speak best by asking meaningful questions and authentically listening. And when it comes to asking questions, we must move beyond simple getting-to-know-you chats and initiate discussions that tap into the spiritual emptiness and longing all humans experience. *Evangelism Outside the Box* author, Rick Richardson, suggested that "We must ask them stimulating, intriguing, even disturbing questions. . . . [such as] Does it make any sense to bring our kids up in a world that is sailing into the future without anchor or rudder? With no reference point outside of ourselves, we are drifting into the shoals of teen violence, sexual disease, environmental disaster, political amorality."[1] As we incorporate true listening and a spirit of genuine understanding into our spiritual conversations, we can move toward an honest, candid discussion of our own relationship with Christ (rather than dishing out a canned gospel "presentation"). According to Richardson, "People are just waiting for you to bring in Jesus in a cliché way. So I often tell how my encounter *with* Jesus blew away all my stereotypes *of* Jesus."[2]

At some point in your efforts to practice evangelism, you'll likely need to plan a time away from your kids in which you can have a sustained spiritual conversation. In the meantime you can still be intentional about initiating conversations (though they may end up being brief) or discussing spiritual matters via e-mail, snail mail, or an evening phone call.

110

> In witnessing, the role of talking is frequently overemphasized. . . . Silence and especially true listening are often the strongest testimony of our faith.
>
> —Dallas Willard

evangelize your children

Don't think you're an evangelist? Think again—you're probably doing evangelism on a daily basis. Your most significant, ultimate supreme, numero-uno evangelism mission is to share your faith with your children. Your children have been given to you as a divine gift, and along with that gift comes an eternity-focused responsibility: introducing your children to Jesus. Ask yourself each day, what can I do to help my children learn about God? feel his love? learn about Jesus' life? understand their need for God? grow to know and trust God? Through conversations, stories, crafts, games, walks in nature, prayers, music, and your example, you can play a central role in helping your children develop faith in Jesus and make a devoted, lifelong commitment to live as Jesus' disciple.

111

a MASH unit for souls

I'm not a big fan of the old '70s show *M*A*S*H*, which was about a Mobile Army Surgical Hospital set in the Korean War era. But the idea of the MASH unit appeals to me because of its spiritual implications. Did you know that the English word *hospital* is at the root of hospitality? Writer Jane Jarrell defined it this way: "Hospitality provides a shelter for the soul, a healing for the spirit. Ultimately this is what we offer when we open our home in the true spirit of love or when we offer our time, gifts or talents outside of our home to reach others."[3] Each of us can live as a MASH unit for souls, choosing to be a shelter and a healing place for all those we encounter. We can extend hospitality and share our faith wherever we go, whether it be at the grocery store, the office, or the library. If home is where the heart is, then as we carry a heart of love with us throughout our day, we can also express a feeling of home—a kindness, openness, and compassion that views strangers as neighbors and that leads spiritual wanderers to their true home in Christ.

talk about it

Discuss these questions with a friend or a small group of other moms.

1. What have been the main barriers you've faced when it comes to practicing evangelism? hospitality?

2. Do you tend to function with a stranger-danger mind-set? How do you generally treat people you don't know? Why?

3. What inspires or challenges you in the story of the woman at the well (John 4:1–42)? What inspires or challenges you from the parable of the Good Samaritan (Luke 10:25–37)?

4. To whom do you feel God may be calling *you* to reach? What next step do you want to take?

5. What other ideas do you have for reaching out (evangelism) and inviting in (hospitality)?

try it

Here are ten ideas you can try.

1. Explore these Scripture passages about evangelism and hospitality: Matthew 25:37–40, 28:16–20; Luke 15:1–32; Acts 1:8, 16:14–15, 18:26; Romans 12:9–13; and Hebrews 13:2. How is God speaking to you through his Word? Journal your thoughts.

2. Identify up to five non-Christians you know or want to start a relationship with, and write down their names. Pray for each one daily, asking God to give you opportunities to begin a friendship, to demonstrate Jesus' love, or to share words of truth.

3. Practice evangelism daily this week by intentionally discussing spiritual matters with each of your children in a fun, age-appropriate fashion.

4. If you have a guest room, straighten it up. Then spend time praying in it, dedicating it to God and inviting him to use it as he sees fit.

5. Step out of your familiar circle of friends and make it a goal to meet one new person this week, such as a coworker in your place of business, a stay-at-home mom at a community event, or a neighbor out for a walk.

113

6. Using the Ignatian model of contemplative reading (see page 77), spend time this week exploring John 4:1–42 (the woman at the well), Luke 10:25–37 (the Good Samaritan), or Matthew 25:31–46 (the sheep and the goats).

7. Cook up some *caritas* love by inviting a non-Christian family over for dinner. Don't feel pressured to discuss spiritual things if it doesn't seem appropriate; your kindness and efforts to establish a friendship will go a long way in showing Jesus' love!

8. If you have a friend who is spiritually hungry, try to schedule a time when the two of you can actually talk. You might get a babysitter so you can meet for coffee, talk while on an exercise walk, or give her a call in the evening once the kids are tucked in. Ask open-ended questions, listen sincerely, share authentically and honestly, and—like the woman at the well—invite your friend to "come, see" Jesus for herself!

9. Use Jane Jarrell's definition of hospitality (on page 111) to craft a prayer in your own words. Write the prayer in your journal and pray it daily, asking God to make these things true in your own life.

10. Get your kids involved in reaching out to your neighborhood by baking cookies, delivering artwork, or purposefully meeting new friends during each visit to the playground.

8

simplicity and stewardship

M ary Brende does her family's laundry with a hand-cranked washing tub. She washes dishes by hand. Her husband, Eric, is a soap maker. They mow their lawn using a hand-powered cutting cylinder. Their three children are schooled in their home. The Brendes don't have a computer, television, or DVD player. They do most of their traveling by foot. No, the Brendes aren't a family from the pages of an early American history book. This family of five lives here and now, smack-dab in downtown St. Louis, Missouri.

When Mary (a former number cruncher) and Eric (an MIT grad) were first married, they decided to try a crazy idea—they moved to an Amish-like community for eighteen months to experience a different style of life (without electricity or running water). Their neighbors helped them learn to farm, pump water by hand, preserve their own food, use kerosene lanterns, and drive horses. This experience of drastic simplicity profoundly changed the young couple. Eric, who's written a book recounting their story called *Better OFF*, felt a profound connection between their minimalist way of living and his experience of God. He wrote, "The way of life we led was inherently contemplative. Since you're surrounded by nature, you're reminded constantly of the glory of God. Working with your hands fosters a contemplative spirit; everything seems to point to God. The harmony you find working with other people—harmonizing your differences—it's indescribable. . . . The whole way of life is sacramental—a physical embodiment of a spiritual reality."[1]

Now, years later and with three kids in tow, Mary and Eric intentionally live a modest, low-tech lifestyle. Along with selling soap at a local farmers market, Eric makes a living driving a bicycle rickshaw. Though they do use electricity for their dehumidifier, small refrigerator, electric fans, and radio, the Brendes choose to walk and bike most of the time and reserve the use of their car only for long trips. Instead of watching television, they play music, interact with friends, or read books. And if they need to use a computer, they bike to the local library. The Brendes have chosen to live this way in the middle of a modern American city in order to maintain the practices of simplicity and stewardship they learned during their year-and-a-half adventure.[2]

It's likely that God isn't calling you to go to such an extreme in the practice of stewardship and simplicity. But this doesn't mean we're off the hook when it comes to these disciplines! If anything, the Brendes' example should cause us each to ask ourselves, "What does it mean for *me* to live simply in our consumeristic society?"

abundant-life values in a never-enough culture

By the time an average American child is five years old, he or she has received 250 toys.[3] That's nearly one toy a week since birth! Almost three-quarters of elementary-school-aged kids have a television in their bedroom,[4] and the stats are almost as stunning for

115

little ones. Thirty-six percent of children ages zero to six have their own TV, 27 percent have their own DVD player or VCR, and one in ten have their own video game system![5] Family psychologist John Rosemond believes this abundance of material possessions can have a devastating effect on children as they grow up to be adults who "are likely to be emotionally stunted, immature people, fixated at a grasping, self-centered stage of development. At the very least, they will tend to confuse the giving and getting of *things* with a deeper and more meaningful level of sharing and trust in relationships."[6] Our kids are growing up in a world in which their friends, television, and perhaps even their parents are reinforcing the message: "You've never got enough. You'd be happier if only you had _____ (fill in the blank with a must-have game or toy)."

And we adults aren't immune to this kiddie consumerism. We not only buy all these things for our children but also model consumeristic values. The average American family carries almost $9,200 in credit card debt[7]—and that doesn't include the loads of money people owe on their new cars, financed entertainment systems, and home equity loans. We just can't seem to get enough!

For a Christian, the main problem with consumerism is not simply that it encourages greed, materialism, or selfish hoarding. Theology professor William T. Cavanaugh hit the nail on the head with this statement:

> The contrast between consumerism and simple living at first glance seems fairly straightforward: Consumerism is about having more stuff, simple living is about having less stuff. . . . [But] consumerism is not so much about having *more* as it is about having *something else*. It is not buying but shopping that captures the spirit of consumerism. Buying is certainly an important part of consumerism, but

buying brings a temporary halt to the restlessness that typifies it. It is this restlessness—the moving on to shopping for something else no matter what one has just purchased—that sets the spiritual tone for consumerism.[8]

In this society, which practices perusing and accumulating stuff as the highest form of popular entertainment, we Christians are called to live by a totally different set of values. Instead of seeking to satiate our inner hunger through shopping, daydreaming about, ordering, or planning for the next material thing, we are to find inner contentment in God alone, embodying the words of St. Augustine: "Our heart is restless until it rests in you."[9]

Jesus' message runs directly counter to the materialistic mantra of our culture. In his Sermon on the Mount, he admonished his followers, "You cannot serve both God and Money" (Matt. 6:24), then exhorted them to live simply, not worrying even about what they will eat or wear because God knows their needs. Couched in the middle of this caution against materialistic worries is that much quoted (and sung) verse: "But seek first his kingdom and his righteousness, and all these things will be given to you as well" (Matt. 6:33). Not only are we not to fritter away our lives by loving and seeking after material things, we're to not even *worry* about them. These concerns don't deserve a second thought when our lives are totally focused on seeking God's kingdom and purposes and the righteousness he intends for our lives. This lifestyle, which is so at odds with our culture's values, isn't barren and dull—it's abundant! Jesus declared, "I have come that they may have life, and have it to the full" (John 10:10).

How can we keep from worrying about the concerns that dominate our culture? How can we live the full, abundant life Christ has for us when we're stuck in the habit of accumulating stuff—especially when we *like* that stuff quite a bit? How can we model for our children the true contentment that can be found in Christ alone instead of displaying the restlessness that pervades our society? We can do that by practicing the spiritual disciplines of simplicity and stewardship.

simplicity and stewardship 101

The spiritual disciplines of simplicity and stewardship both focus on how we value, relate to, and use things: money, possessions, and the material world. Christ-honoring simplicity is reflected in our outward choices, but it reveals an inner attitude of unswerving trust in God as our provider. Richard Foster proposed that simplicity is "a way of living in which everything we have we received as a gift, and everything we have is cared for by God, and everything we have is available to others when it is right and good."[10]

For many people the idea of stewardship is most often associated with giving financially to the church. This practice is definitely important in the life of every Christian, but there is far more to stewardship than just putting money in the offering plate. To practice the discipline of stewardship means that instead of viewing our money and our things as *ours*, we see ourselves as stewards—meaning managers or trustees—of the things that belong to God but which he has entrusted to us. As stewards, we seek to live as God-honoring caretakers not only of our money but also of our talents, our children, our time, our fellow human beings, and the created world. Theology professor R. Paul Stevens insightfully described stewardship as "manag[ing] God's world in harmony with the owner's mind."[11] As

> Jesus Christ and all the writers of the New Testament call us to break free of mammon lust and live in joyous trust. Their radical criticism of wealth is combined with a spirit of unconditional generosity.
>
> —Richard Foster

Jesus emphasized in the parable of the talents in Matthew 25:14–30, rather than living in a way that hoards, uses up, or wastes resources purely for our own pleasure, comfort, or self-protection, we should seek to enjoy, care for, and use material things in a way that brings glory to God and reflects the values of God's kingdom. When we practice simplicity and stewardship, we

- Reject the consumerist values and addictions of our culture.
- Find true contentment in Christ rather than in acquiring things, and we demonstrate that contentment through our joy.
- Recognize our sinful tendency to acquire and hold on to too much stuff and instead choose to live selflessly.
- Take practical action steps to modify our lifestyle to reflect God's perspective on money and possessions.
- Wisely use the resources God has given us for his purposes by giving generously, sacrificially, and cheerfully.
- Renounce and refuse to materially support unjust businesses, practices, and values that exacerbate the problems of disenfranchisement and poverty.
- Honor God by caring for his creation (both the natural world and human beings).

119

putting it into action: mom-friendly ideas

Choosing to practice simplicity and stewardship probably won't mean that you'll reject all technology, renounce money entirely (as some early Christians did), or give up your home and possessions so that you and your family can live in a cave. But it will mean making some extremely difficult decisions about the way you choose to live. Your kids are watching you, learning from your example how they should value money and material things. Here are just a few ways to renovate your relationship with your stuff and build a solid foundation for your children on what truly satisfies.

take a look at your lifestyle

The first and often most challenging step in practicing simplicity and stewardship is to take a hard look at the way you live. With an open heart, ask yourself, "Do we have too much stuff? Do we spend too much time or money on shopping or on entertaining ourselves? Does the way we use our time reflect what is truly important to our family? Does the way we handle our money reflect God's values?" Every single one of us, if we're brutally honest, will likely respond to these questions with the admission that we need to make some changes. Talk to your family members or a trusted Christian friend about your thoughts. Then implement some practical action steps. For example, as a family you may decide to cut some activities out of your calendar in order to spend more time together. Or you may decide it's time to revise the family budget so that it reflects principles of simple living, financial stewardship, and sacrificial giving.

[A]nyone who professes to be a disciple must demonstrate the reality of that profession by transformed living, including in the areas of personal spending and giving. . . . [T]he person who never displays any concern for the Lord's work and for the poor and who never gives anything to help them by definition is not someone whom the power of the Spirit has touched."

—Craig L. Blomberg

break the accumulation cycle

When attempting to simplify your lifestyle, it is important to mute the culture's message that you never have enough. You can do this by taking some practical action steps with your kids that will clear your minds of consumerist values and clear your house of excess possessions. A great way to do this is to make your home a commercial-free zone. Advertisements on television, radio, and magazines incessantly repeat the lie that you or your kids will be happy only when you add another thing to your life. No matter how hard you try, you won't be able to foster a simplicity mind-set with these destructive messages constantly chirping in the background. Do what you can to keep commercials out of your home. You can mute the TV or radio (or turn it off) during commercials. While there's no way to avoid driving past the huge billboards that line the road, you can help kids develop an advertisement immunity by occasionally pointing them out to your children and discussing their influence. You might say, "See that sign about hamburgers? It's trying to make you feel hungry so you go to that restaurant. Isn't it funny how a silly picture is trying to trick us into feeling hungry?" By quieting the voices that tell us we never have enough, we're more easily able to hear Christ's message to us: "I am enough" (see 2 Corinthians 12:9).

121

There are lots of methods for paring down the pile of things that seems to surreptitiously grow in our homes. Here are a few.

Get One, Give One. A couple of days after a holiday, sit down with your child and explain, "Now that we have some new toys (or clothes or books), we can give away some of our other things to kids that don't have any." Then sort through your child's toys together and gently help him or her decide on a few items to part with. (Be sure to let your child also see you sort out some of your own things to give away.) It's not important that you give away the exact number of items that you've received; the real value is helping your family stay free of that dangerous habit of accumulating more and more stuff.

Do Some Spring Cleaning. Choose a day in the spring (or in any season) on which your family will take stock of all the things in your house and together select the items you can give to those in need. Make the day fun for your kids by playing upbeat music as you clean, then top off the day with pizza and ice cream. Talk together as a family about how you can show God's love through all the items you're getting rid of, and decide together on a local nonprofit organization to donate the materials to.

Have a Garage Sale with a Purpose. Instead of keeping the money your family makes from selling garage sale items, decide together on a ministry to which your family can donate the proceeds. Post signs letting customers know who will receive the income. Rather than bartering for a cheaper price, some customers may donate a few extra dollars to help a good cause.

give sacrificially

My three-year-old son and I were doing some spring cleaning by sorting through a gigantic pile of stuffed animals. On the previous Sunday at church, Davis had learned about sharing with those in need, and I immediately (and sneakily) saw it as an opportunity to clear out some space in his closet. We talked about how some little kids don't have any toys, and some don't even have a place to live. "Would you like to give away some of your toys to kids who don't have any?" I asked.

"Yes!" he answered enthusiastically.

I felt very spiritual as he sat on my lap and I guided him in sorting out his stuffed animals into "keep" and "giveaway" piles. As we narrowed down to a final few items, I noticed a green puppy dog he's loved since infancy. "OK, Davis," I said, "why don't you look at the pile we've got left and see if there are any favorite toys there." Immediately he picked up the green puppy and gave it a big hug. "This is my favorite!" he said. I was relieved that he had identified it so we could avoid a future nighttime meltdown in which he cried for the now permanently missing toy. But then he tossed the dog on top of the giveaway pile.

"Wait, Davis," I said as I picked up the dog and handed it back to him. "I thought this was a favorite. Don't you want to keep it?"

"Yes, it's my favorite," he said, matter-of-factly, tossing it back onto the giveaway pile. "I want to give it to a kid who doesn't have a favorite."

123

Boy, did I feel convicted! The sacrificial giving that is usually a struggle for me was a natural reaction for my son. He understood at a basic level that giving isn't simply a way to get rid of unwanted junk but is an opportunity to bless someone by offering our best. Giving is meaningful only when it costs us something. When giving is purely mechanical, it means nothing.

Two women in the New Testament exemplify sacrificial giving. Mary of Bethany anointed Jesus' feet with expensive perfume as a lavish act of worship (John 12:1–8). The perfume she lovingly gave to Jesus was worth a year's wages! An even greater sacrifice was made by a poor widow who gave two small coins (worth less than a penny) as her offering to God; Jesus pointed out that this woman "put in everything—all she had to live on" (Mark 12:44). She didn't have a secret stash set aside for herself; she gave the entirety of her financial assets to God. What amazing examples!

> I give you all my worldly goods. May I prize them and use them only for you. May I faithfully restore to you, in the poor, all you have entrusted me with, above the necessaries of life; and be content to part with them too, whenever you, my Lord, shall require them at my hands.
>
> —John Wesley

When we look at material things from a radically kingdom-focused perspective, we see our money and possession as *God's* money and possessions, and we cheerfully invite him to use them as he will. We can practice good stewardship by regularly contributing money to our church, to local or international ministries, or for the support of missionaries. Older kids can participate by regularly giving a portion of their allowance money. And to help our little ones understand sacrificial giving (or the other way around, as it was in my case!), we can regularly give away material things. Young kids won't understand the concept of giving money, but they *will* understand when you take them to your closet and pick out a few favorite outfits and explain that you'll be giving them to others who need them. As you practice the get-one-give-one principle or do your spring cleaning, you can give away some nice things that are hard to part with to emphasize the idea that we sacrifice our wants for God's greater purposes.

care for god's creation

One of the most valuable resources God has entrusted to us is his beautiful creation: the amazing planet he made and, even more valuable, the human beings God created to inhabit it. Sadly, we Christians often fail to take our caretaking responsibilities seriously. We live in a world in which more than sixteen thousand children die from hunger-related causes each day[12] and workers around the globe labor in sweatshops, earning barely enough to buy food for their families. As the wealth in Western countries like ours balloons, third-world economies struggle along in a cycle of debt, poverty, and disenfranchisement. Pollution and waste contribute not only to illnesses and death among the poor but also to the slow destruction of plant and animal species and awesome natural wonders God created.

Though we can't change the world's economic and environmental realities on our own, practicing simplicity and God-honoring stewardship "enables us to live lives of integrity in the face of the terrible realities of our global village."[13] As caretakers of our fellow human beings, we can choose to refrain from participating in unjust business systems that exacerbate poverty by paying third-world growers and workers a pittance while profiting greatly when the products are sold in Western countries. Instead, when we're gift-buying or picking up next week's supply of java, we can choose to support fair trade organizations that aim to pay their workers a living wage—a just amount that enables the workers to provide adequately for their families' health and well-being. (To find out more about these issues, see the Resources section of this book.)

125

When it comes to caring for the earth, there are lots of easy and fun ways you can model stewardship for your kids, teaching them from a young age how they can honor God by celebrating and enjoying the incredible world he made.

Plant a Garden. Open your kids' eyes to the wonder of God's world by planting and caring for a simple garden together. Little ones often love to dig their hands into the dirt to plant seeds and pull weeds. As you garden together, you can talk about how God gave Adam and Eve the job of caring for the garden of Eden, and you can discuss God's power to turn a little seed into a carrot,

> [T]he first Christians were clearly and consistently generous in giving from their wealth and concerned to impact unjust social structures as well as to alleviate personal suffering.
>
> —Craig L. Blomberg

or you can notice God's artwork in the details of leaves and tiny bugs. Later, when you harvest your veggies together, you can say prayers of thanks aloud. These special moments with you will help your kids develop an inherent appreciation for God's good earth.

Conserve Resources. Work together as a family to cut energy costs, reduce waste, and recycle. Little ones can learn how to sort glass, paper, and plastic from other trash items. You can even make a game out of it by, for example, having your kids shoot baskets with empty pop cans. Explain to your kids the basic concept of recycling and let them know that reducing our waste is a way to show God how thankful we are for the special world he made for us.

Clean Up the Neighborhood. Have fun as a family cleaning up parks or trails near your home. (For more about this idea, see page 92).

all the vain things

In 1707, hymn writer Isaac Watts penned these compelling words:

> When I survey the wondrous cross
> On which the Prince of Glory died,
> My richest gain I count but loss,
> And pour contempt on all my pride . . .
> All the vain things that charm me most,
> I sacrifice them to His blood . . .
> Were the whole realm of nature mine,
> That were a present far too small;
> Love so amazing, so divine,
> Demands my soul, my life, my all![14]

As Watts so clearly understood, when we grow closer to Christ as his disciple, our perspective on material things necessarily changes. Instead of always seeking after the next new thing, we passionately seek him. Rather than worrying about our finances, our clothing, or how we can keep up with the Joneses, our hearts find rest and purpose in him. No longer surrounding ourselves with more and more things in a doomed effort to fill our emptiness, we seek to follow Jesus' example by emptying ourselves of our own selfish desires. As we focus on the cross, our proper relationship with material things comes into clearer focus. As we practice simplicity and stewardship and model it for our children, we demonstrate what is truly important in our lives: Christ, and Christ alone.

talk about it

Discuss these questions with a friend or a small group of other moms.

1. Does the lifestyle of the Brendes'—or of Christians who practice extreme simplicity, such as the Amish—appeal to you? Why or why not?

2. Have you felt the influence of consumerism in your life? How do you think consumerism impacts spiritual growth?

3. What do you think the phrase "life to the full" (John 10:10) really means? What place should money and possessions have in the abundant life?

4. How do you respond to the examples of sacrificial giving seen in Mary (John 12:1–8) and the poor widow (Mark 12:41–44)? Do you think God calls all of us to live and give in this way?

5. How do you think practicing simplicity and stewardship could positively impact your spiritual life? your family's life? Be specific.

try it

Here are ten ideas you can try.

1. Read these passages about simplicity and stewardship: Genesis 1:27–31, 2:15; Psalm 24:1, 50:10; Isaiah 1:15–17; Amos 5:11–14; Matthew 6:11, 6:19–34, 8:19–20, 16:26, 25:14–30; Mark 12:41–44; and John 12:1–8. How can you apply them to your daily living? Journal your thoughts.

2. Grab a pen and paper and use it to take an inventory both of your family's "stuff" and of the way you spend time. Write down ideas about things you need to change. Then talk them through with your family or a close Christian friend.

3. Ban commercials from your house for a week. Then reflect on how your perspective on what you really "need" has changed.

4. Tell your children the story of the poor widow (Mark 12:41–44) and invite them to share ideas about how your family can apply the story's principles together.

5. Do some spring cleaning with your kids (even if it's not spring!) and identify specific toys and other items your family can give to those in need.

6. Set time aside as a family to enjoy God's good creation by doing something outdoors, such as going on a walk or cloud gazing. Use the opportunity to talk to your kids about what things damage God's earth and the steps your family can take to help care for the world God made.

7. Memorize Saint Augustine's prayer (page 117) or John Wesley's prayer (page 123) and include it in your daily prayer time for a week.

8. If your family struggles with the way you handle money, ask your pastor to refer you to someone who can confidentially help you develop a family budget built on the biblical principles of tithing, simplicity, and sacrificial giving.

9. Work with your kids to make a list of your family's wants and needs. Then talk about the difference together.

10. Sing "When I Survey the Wondrous Cross" during a time alone with God. Then meditate on the words.

9

fasting

A few weeks earlier, my doctor had given me the bad news: I had failed the one-hour glucose test that's a routine part of prenatal testing. (You know the test: it's the one where you have to down a bottle of liquid that tastes like a melted orange Popsicle with orange Kool-Aid and flat orange pop mixed in.) Now I was in the hospital waiting room, halfway through the dreaded *three-hour* glucose test. I don't know who invented this ghastly experiment, but it must have been someone with a sick sense of humor. Requiring a woman who is seven months pregnant to fast is like asking a tyrannosaurus to eat only vegetables: It's absolutely nuts!

I had been required to skip only breakfast, but by 9:00 a.m., others in the waiting room could hear the loud growls coming from my protruding stomach. By ten o'clock my eyes had glazed over and all I could think about was donuts. By eleven o'clock I had curled into the fetal position on a waiting room couch and was murmuring, "How can they call this a fast? This is the slowest that time has ever passed in my entire life!" At noon, after they had checked my blood a final time, I stumbled to the car and drove one block to the nearest fast-food restaurant, then scarfed down a large order of jalepeño poppers and French fries. (This is not my usual diet—remember that I was certifiably insane by this point.) I remember thinking (while still under the influence of my bizarre lunch) that this experience of fasting, undertaken only for medical reasons, had been total torture. I wondered why anyone would choose to do this if they didn't absolutely have to. How could this crazy behavior be considered a spiritual discipline?

the least favorite discipline

In my recent and completely unscientific survey of busy-mom friends, fasting rose to the top as the unrivaled winner of the coveted Spiritual Discipline Least Compatible with My Real Life award. This isn't because busy moms have ravenous appetites or a treatment-worthy addiction to chocolate. It's because fasting from food simply isn't a healthy choice for pregnant or nursing moms. And even for those who aren't pregnant or nursing, fasting from food can be a real problem because of the superhuman degree of stamina motherhood often demands. As one friend put it, "I didn't realize before I had my son how much energy it would require—mothering is a full contact sport!" As moms, we have the responsibility of teaching and modeling healthy eating habits for our children; little kids are likely to misunderstand why Mommy isn't eating lunch and could actually develop dangerously unhealthy ideas regarding eating (or not eating) when they misunderstand Mommy's choice to abstain from a meal. It is also pretty difficult to pray fervently as a part of fasting when you're sitting with your children and monitoring their macaroni consumption! One mom of three was brutally honest with me about the reason she avoids fasting: "The effect of fasting on me is not something I would want to subject my children to. I am not a nice person when I feel as bad as I do when I've gone without food." I can relate to that!

Yet, as writer Keith Drury pointed out in his book *With Unveiled Faces*, in both the Old Testament and in Jesus' time, fasting was an accepted, normative part of Jewish and Christian life: "[I]t was assumed that people practiced this discipline, and ever since then it has been assumed that fasting is an important part of the Christian lifestyle. Until recently, that is. Only in contemporary times have Christians concluded that prayer and Bible reading are required but that fasting is optional."[1] Fasting and parallel acts of self-denial are *not* optional disciplines, no matter how much we'd like to treat them that way! Though Jesus never set strict guidelines for how and when his followers should fast, he modeled fasting himself by beginning his earthly ministry with a forty-day fast (Matt. 4:1–11) and taught about fasting in a way that assumed that his disciples would practice it (6:16).

Not only is fasting treated as normative in Scripture, but God's Word is equally clear that fasting is not a lone-ranger discipline; it is intimately connected with other spiritual practices. In the Bible, fasting is nearly always accompanied by prayer. Fasting is often an immediate response by those who through self-examination are led to mourning and repentance over sin. Fasting is also an extension of the discipline of simplicity; by denying ourselves the ability to satisfy an appetite (whether it be for food, things, or an activity), we're able to narrow our focus on our soul's true hunger for intimacy with God. The Bible teaches clearly that fasting must also be partnered with service, hospitality, and stewardship of our fellow human beings; in fact, fasting means nothing to God if it is not accompanied by true worship, exhibited by caring for those in need. Through his prophet Isaiah, God harshly rebuked those who'd made a show of elaborate religious fasting but neglected to show love in action to those in need: "Is not this the kind of fasting I have chosen: to loose the chains of injustice and untie the cords of the yoke, to set the oppressed free and break every yoke? Is it not to share your food with the hungry and to provide the poor wanderer with shelter—when you see the naked, to clothe him, and not to turn away from your own flesh and blood?" (Isa. 58:6–7).

In addition to the example of Jesus, there are many other accounts of fasting in the Bible. Here are two fasting experiences of women from different walks of life. In the Old Testament we encounter Esther, who is young, beautiful, and in the middle of a life-threatening crisis. Esther has been chosen to marry a pagan king who had recently gotten rid of his previous wife. When Esther is informed of an edict that would result in the genocide of her people, she devotes three days to fasting and prayer and is joined by all the Jews in her city. Through this intense time of focusing her energy, hunger, and entire being on God, Esther finds the strength and courage to do what God has called her to do: risk her life in order to protect her people.

Early in the New Testament, we encounter another awesome portrait of fasting in Anna. A widow, at least eighty-four years old, Anna lives in the Temple and spends her time "worshiping with fasting and prayer night and day" (Luke 2:37 ESV). Her fasting and prayer are born from her utter devotion to God. As a result of her connection to God, Anna is able to clearly sense God's leading and hear his voice. Prompted by God's Spirit, she recognizes the infant Jesus as the promised Messiah! Anna was one of the very first witnesses to the gospel, "speak[ing] of him to all who were waiting for the redemption of Jerusalem" (verse 38 ESV).

Like these godly women, we can commune with God in a special way when we practice fasting and self-denial as part of our worship and prayer. When we practice the discipline of fasting, we

133

Focus on God. By putting aside the distractions of our appetites for other things, we are able to focus more directly on our relationship with God.

Pray Fervently. Fasting creates an increased sense of our dependence on God and allows us to pray more openly and sincerely.

Experience Satisfaction. Through fasting we discover the true soul satisfaction that can be found only when we "feast" on God's presence.

Worship God. By offering the gift of our sacrifice to God, we engage in an act of true worship.

Gain Spiritual Insight. As we abstain from food, things, or some other activity, we come to recognize the destructive power of our appetites, cravings, temptations, and habits. We come face-to-face with our own weakness in resisting temptation and get an accurate picture of how much we need God's help to live rightly.

> More than any other Discipline, fasting reveals the things that control us.
>
> —Richard Foster

Break Harmful Appetites. Because fasting forces us to find perspective and power through the Holy Spirit, it enables us to break free of spiritually hurtful habits and appetites.

Mature Spiritually. We develop a Christlike mind-set and grow in spiritual maturity when we fast. In a sermon on fasting, John Wesley explained, "And it is chiefly, as it is an help to prayer, that [fasting] has so frequently been found a means, in the hand of God, of confirming and increasing, not [only] one virtue [chastity], . . . but also seriousness of spirit, earnestness, sensibility and tenderness of conscience, deadness to the world, and consequently the love of God, and every holy and heavenly affection."[2]

Prepare to Serve. We are strengthened and prepared to joyfully serve and obey Christ when we deny ourselves through fasting. Dietrich Bonhoeffer, a German pastor who was executed by the

Nazis during World War II, explained that the central purpose of fasting should be "to make the disciples more ready and cheerful to accomplish those things which God would have done. Fasting helps to discipline the self-indulgent and slothful will which is so reluctant to serve the Lord . . . When the flesh is satisfied it is hard to pray with cheerfulness or to devote oneself to a life of service which calls for much self-renunciation."[3]

putting it into action: mom-friendly ideas

If you're like most of the moms I know, you probably would have cast your vote for fasting to be named the Spiritual Discipline Least Compatible with My Real Life. Though complete fasting from food does involve hurdles that some of us just can't overcome, there are several meaningful ways you can practice fasting and self-denial without endangering your health, exhausting your energy supply, or confusing your kids. (Self-denial is always tough, however, so I can't make any guarantees about avoiding a bad mood—that's up to you.)

give up a meal

Since fasting from food is the primary form of fasting spoken about in Scripture, we do ourselves a disservice if we skip over this type of fasting entirely. Fasting from food can take many forms. Absolute fasting, in which a person temporarily gives up eating altogether, can involve fasting for one meal or for as long as several days. Shelly, a mom I know, has committed to fast from food for one day a year; she makes arrangements ahead of time

> "He humbled you, causing you to hunger and then feeding you with manna...to teach you that man does not live on bread alone but on every word that comes from the mouth of the LORD."
>
> —Deuteronomy 8:3

for her husband to watch the kids, then spends a day on her own mini-retreat of prayer, fasting, and worship. Though once a year might not seem often to some, I admire my friend's determination to make this happen; she has found that this one day of fasting has a significant spiritual impact on her entire year. Is there a time when you could get away from your kids for one meal, whether it be at work or by arranging for a babysitter? Your kids won't know you didn't eat, so they won't be confused—and you'll be able to have a little peace and quiet so you can pray!

abstain from certain foods

Abstinence fasting is a very doable way of fasting that even pregnant and nursing moms can practice. In abstinence fasting, you choose to give up a certain type of food for a set period of time. For example, you may choose to do without something you really crave, such as chocolate, soda pop, coffee, desserts, pizza, or even meat (if it is replaced with other healthy sources of protein). You may be surprised to discover that giving up a favorite food can be even harder than giving up food altogether!

fast from things

In our consumerist society, we all have powerful appetites for things beyond food; sometimes these habits have even become addictions without us realizing it—addictions to entertainment, to busyness, to pleasure. In her *Spiritual Disciplines Handbook*, Adele Ahlberg Calhoun wrote that "fasting is an opportunity to lay down an appetite—an appetite for food, for media, for shopping. This act of self-denial may not seem huge—it's just a meal or a trip to the mall—but it brings us face to face with the hunger at the core of our being. Fasting exposes how we try to keep empty hunger at bay and gain a sense of well being by devouring creature comforts."[4] We can practice the principle of fasting by denying ourselves the satisfaction of an appetite or foregoing a habit (good or bad) that distracts our focus from God. We can fast from

- Media consumption (things like television, movies, radio, CDs, or MP3 players).
- Communication (such as talking on the telephone, sending instant messages or e-mail, or Web surfing).

137

- Time-consuming hobbies (like scrapbooking, sewing, or gardening).
- Shopping (including window shopping).
- Appearance luxuries (such as jewelry or makeup).
- Sexual intimacy (see 1 Corinthians 7:3–5).
- Reading (including books, the newspaper, magazines, or Web pages).
- Working out (if you're an exercise junkie).
- Using modern conveniences (like elevators, microwaves, dishwashers, or driving the car).

The possibilities are endless; the important thing is that your fast be a legitimate act of self-denial. In other words, if you already don't exercise, fasting from working out isn't much of a sacrifice! In her book *Girl Meets God*, Ph.D. student and confessed bibliophile Lauren Winner described the challenge she received from her pastor to give up something really meaningful during Lent: reading. He knew that reading was more than a hobby for Winner—it was a passion. She balked at the idea at first, but Winner eventually decided to give up books for her Lenten fast. Though she did "cheat" a few times, she still found the experience profoundly impactful. She wrote, "Giving up books for six weeks did not just leave me more free time. It did not just save me some money. It also left me starkly alone with my life . . . During Lent, I don't have that always-cure, and I find myself, not surprisingly, praying more. At first I pray more because I have time on my hands . . . But I also find myself praying more because I don't have my usual distractions. When I am stuck in a puddle of sadness and mistakes, I can't take them to Mitford [the setting for her favorite books]. I have to take them to God."[5]

> If we are to grow in faithful living, we need to renounce the things that choke off the fullness of life that God intended for us. . . . We must learn the practice of saying no to that which crowds God out and yes to a way of life that makes space for God.
>
> —M. Shawn Copeland

What favorite thing can you give up to God as a gift for a period of fasting? What appetite or habit has too much power over you? Are you willing to surrender it to God through a set time of self-denial? You may undertake some of these fasts for only a day, while at other times God may lead you to fast for a month or more. Seek God's voice; the Holy Spirit will guide you in your sincere effort to practice the discipline of fasting.

forego something permanently

At times God may tug at your heart about an issue and call you to go one step beyond a temporary fast; he may want you to give up a behavior, destructive habit, or spiritual distraction altogether. In some cases, the need for a permanent commitment of self-denial (a practice called renunciation) is obvious, as in Christians who are addicted to alcohol or who are tempted by Internet pornography. But God doesn't call us to forego only obvious sins. At times he may call us individually to let go of certain practices for his own purposes in order to advance our spiritual growth. For example, God may call you to stop

138

watching a favorite television show that has questionable content. Or perhaps God wants you to give up a gluttonous behavior such as consumption of sweets. Or God may want you to renounce patterns of speech such as sarcasm, gossip, coarse joking, or judgmental comments. God may even call you to forego a relationship that has a continually negative effect on your spiritual life.

Dietrich Bonhoeffer once wrote that "it is imperative for the Christian to achieve renunciation, to practise [sic] self-effacement, to distinguish his life from the life of the world."[6] Some Christians have taken renunciation too far by pulling back entirely from all things they deem "worldly" (including relationships with non-Christians). We should avoid that extreme practice, but we *can* practice renunciation in a healthy, appropriate, and balanced way by remaining attentive and obedient to the Holy Spirit's leading. Through prayer and an open and willing heart, you can continually ask God to reveal to you habits or behaviors that he wants you to say a permanent no to in order to make space for the renovation he longs to accomplish in your life.

sharpening the senses

Scientific studies demonstrate that when a person is bereft of one sense (such as sight or hearing), the other senses seem to be sharpened. For example, blind people often have an acutely developed sense of hearing—far beyond that of an average sighted person—and are able to discern amazing details such as how many people are nearby or the approximate size of a room. Similarly, the deaf often observe visual details at a pace well beyond hearing people; they can do things such as read lips, decipher sign language from far away, and recall small items that others tend to overlook.

A young girl named Fanny Crosby grew up in New York in the 1820s and '30's. From infancy Fanny was completely blind. But her blindness did not hold her back in life; she became one of America's great Christian artists, composing more than nine thousand poems and songs. Fanny's strengthened awareness through hearing (due to her blindness) certainly contributed to her success as a musician, but what is even more profound is the way her physical deprivation strengthened and sharpened her *spiritual* sight.

Once someone commented that it was a shame that Fanny, who possessed so many talents, had to struggle with blindness. Fanny's response floors me. She said, "Do you know that if at birth I had been able to make one petition, it would have been that I should be born blind?" She went on to explain, "Because when I get to heaven, the first face that shall ever gladden my sight will be that of my Savior!"[7] What an amazing example of devotion! Fanny believed that her faith—her passionate desire to see and to love Jesus—was directly impacted by her inability to see the physical world. Though she did not choose to give up her sense of sight (even though she apparently would have), her deprivation in this one area of physical life allowed her to experience a focused and intense spiritual reality in a way she might not have if she had been sighted.

When we give up something from our physical life through the discipline of fasting, we experience this same spiritual truth in a small way. The deprivation we undergo in one area of our lives enables us to sharpen and strengthen our spiritual life—our sense of hearing God, our awareness of his presence, our willingness and desire to pray, our sense of satisfaction and contentment found only in him, our deep and steadfast love for God. As we practice the discipline of fasting, may we sing along with the psalmist,

As the deer pants for streams of water,
so my soul pants for you, O God.
My soul thirsts for God, for the living God.

—Psalm 42:1–2

talk about it

*Discuss these questions with a friend or a small group of
other moms.*

1. Before you read this chapter, did you consider the discipline of
   fasting to be incompatible with your life as a busy mom? What
   do you think about it now?
2. Why do you think Christians today often treat fasting as optional?
   What attitudes and feelings might be behind this mind-set?
3. In your own words, why is fasting an important spiritual discipline? What does it accomplish?
4. How do Jesus, Esther, and Anna's examples of fasting inspire
   or challenge you?
5. What is something meaningful that you could fast from?

try it

Here are ten ideas you can try.

1. Read these passages about fasting: Deuteronomy 8:3; 1 Samuel
   7:5–6; Esther 3:12–5:2; Isaiah 58:1–10; Matthew 6:16–18, 16:24;
   Luke 2:22–38; Acts 13:1–3, and 14:23. What insights do they
   give you about the purposes of fasting? Journal your thoughts.

2. Identify an upcoming mealtime when you'll be away from your children (whether it's while you're at work or at a time when you'll need to arrange for a babysitter). Fast from that meal and spend time praying and meditating on God's Word.

3. If you're unable to fast from a meal due to health reasons, select a favorite food to abstain from for a set period of time. Each time you crave that food, turn to God in prayer and praise instead of indulging your appetite.

4. If you know someone who regularly practices the discipline of fasting, invite that person to talk with you about the role fasting has had on his or her spiritual growth. What struggles has it involved? What impact has fasting had on the prayer life or other aspects of that person's faith? What practical or spiritual advice about fasting could he or she share with you?

5. Grab a hymnal and read or sing a Fanny Crosby hymn (several will likely be listed in the index of authors or composers). Consider how the lyrics exemplify her sharpened spiritual sight, and contemplate the impact experiences of self-denial could have on your own spiritual perspective.

6. Invite a friend to fast along with you for one month, whether it be from a specific meal (such as lunch on Wednesdays), a favorite food (perhaps chocolate), or an activity (such as watching television). Hold each other accountable, encourage each other, and pray for each other during the process.

7. Study Jesus' fast in the wilderness. (See Matthew 4:1–11.) What strength and insight do you gain from his example as you prepare to begin a fast of your own?

8. Identify a habit or activity you'd be willing to fast from for a set period of time. Then make a spiritual commitment. Write your specific commitment here.

_____

_____

_____

_____

_____

9. Memorize Psalm 42:1–2. Then meditate on it each day this week.

10. Reread M. Shawn Copeland's quote on page 138. Then flip back through this book and reflect on what you've read and thought about so far. What practices has God been leading you to say yes to in order to develop a way of life that has space for him? What habits, behaviors, or attitudes that crowd God out has he been prompting you to say no to? Pray about your conclusions.

10

fellowship

We started attending our church when our son Elijah was six weeks old," explained my friend Amie when I asked about her efforts to develop friendships after moving to a new city. She found her new church welcoming, but she also encountered the odd relationship pattern that many moms experience. "Sometimes it feels like Elijah is a distraction from fellowship," she related. "It's like having a conversation piece glued to my side. People are always fascinated with him, and they constantly pinch his cheeks and give me advice. Is this how a weatherman feels on a blind date? 'No, I'd really like to talk about something other than the weather, thanks.'"

Ever felt that way? It's great to talk about our kids, but there's more to us than our adorable offspring! Authentic fellowship is something Christian moms desperately need, but it's not easy to find in our society of comfortable distances. Amie continued: "We all have conversational lifejackets that we use to keep us from getting in too deep. They keep us floating on the surface—and that's OK sometimes. Every conversation doesn't need to feel as if you're talking with your therapist. But we also need relationships where we can be real and honest."

Fellowship is more than the half-hour coffee and banana bread time between church services. And we know deep down that God created us to have something more than surfacy acquaintanceship or cliquish friendships. But what is fellowship as a spiritual discipline? And how is a busy mom to practice it when sustained adult conversations of any kind are on the endangered species list in our spiritual lives?

145

god's instrument for growth

We live in an increasingly isolated society. People come home from work, pull into their garages, go inside, and *stay* inside, never meeting their neighbors or interacting with anyone but their coworkers and immediate family members. Television characters have replaced real friends. Internet chats have usurped the place of face-to-face conversations. What's worse, we actually *like* this feeling of anonymity—having the freedom to make our own decisions, guard our privacy, and carefully choose who (if anyone) to allow into our fenced-off world.

Sadly, as Christians we often live in the same state of isolation. Whether it is by choice or as a result of circumstances, many of us try to "go it alone" when it comes to spiritual growth. Sure, we have friends who are Christians, but we rarely (if ever) open up to them about the struggles in our effort to follow Christ. We rely on the Holy Spirit and our own gumption to grow—or at least to keep up the appearance of growing.

But God designed us to *need* community. From the first man Adam all the way down to each of us, it is "not good" for human beings to do life alone. We need friends, mentors, and spiritual brothers and sisters not just to meet an emotional need but also, and more important, to help us grow as disciples in Christ. Scripture affirms this truth in Proverbs 27:17 (TNIV): "As iron sharpens iron, so one person sharpens another." When we live isolated lives, absent of real fellowship, we relinquish the very tool God would use to prod us along in growing as disciples of Jesus. Within the context of fellowship, we are enabled to faithfully practice the other spiritual disciplines, share our experiences, encourage and support one another through the Holy Spirit, and be "sharpened" in our faith.

> God never makes private, secret salvation deals with people. His relationships with us are personal, true, intimate, yes; but private, no. We are a family in Christ. When we become Christians, we are among brothers and sisters in faith. No Christian is an only child.
>
> —Eugene Peterson

146

God not only designed us for fellowship but also placed us in a community the moment we began a faith relationship with Jesus. Whether we were aware of it or not, we immediately became an indispensable part of God's Church. And being made part of the Church is accompanied by a *commitment*. We are not our own, our lives are not all about us, and living as lone-ranger Christians simply isn't an option. Your spiritual life as a Jesus follower cannot survive or thrive in isolation. As the Apostle Paul put it, "Just as each of us has one body with many members . . . so in Christ we who are many form one body, and *each member belongs to all the others*" (Rom. 12:4–6, emphasis added).

The term *fellowship* comes from the New Testament word *koinonia,* which essentially means joint participation. When we fellowship with others, we join in their lives, we share a common mission, we participate together in the work of God's Church on earth.

As we practice the discipline of fellowship, we

- *Recognize* that God designed us to grow in community with others.
- *Enjoy* and delight in the good gift of friendship.
- *Extend* grace to other Christians who have wronged us or think differently than we do.
- *Preserve* the unity of the Church and seek to overcome any of our own sinful tendencies that threaten this unity.
- *Offer* our spiritual gifts and strengths to others.
- *Determine* to confess our sins, vulnerabilities, and weaknesses to other Christians who can aid us in our spiritual growth.
- *Open* ourselves to hear and follow God's direction revealed to us through brothers and sisters in Christ.

putting it into action: mom-friendly ideas

Motherhood is a tough season of life for creating fellowship, but this discipline is essential to our lives and must be pursued at almost any cost. Here are a few ways you can build fellowship into the framework of your life.

be content with kid time

Christin and her husband are leaders of a small group that meets in their home. After a particularly busy week, Christin was looking forward to time with adult friends and the creative spiritual experience she and her husband had planned. But things didn't turn out quite as she expected.

We had planned a time of journaling to process what we'd been learning the past year and what we wanted to learn about God in the year to come. Our children were upstairs watching a movie; but about three minutes into the journaling experience, our two-year-old (who is being potty trained) called downstairs that she needed help using the bathroom.

I went upstairs and discovered that she didn't want to go potty; she just wanted me to spend time with her. I ended up playing a game with her while the others journaled. It was hard to give up the opportunity to fellowship that I'd been looking forward to—but I really enjoyed that time with my daughter and found it refreshing.

One thing that impresses and convicts me about Christin is that she doesn't resort to the common but extremely limited perspective on fellowship that I often have: namely that it consists only of significant, uninterrupted conversations and growth with other Christian adults. Her viewpoint is refreshing: "My practice of Christian disciplines can't happen apart from community, and community includes my children. They show me my weaknesses; they show me what childlike faith looks like. They pray for me and with me and are a part of every joy and sorrow I experience."

Hanging out with kids all the time can feel isolating and lonely— but Christin's right: We can fellowship with our children. Certainly we won't have deep, grown-up conversations with them, but we can share in the Christian life with them. Next time you're longing for interaction time with friends, ask God to help you be content in the moment with your children; invite him to help you learn from them and grow in faith as a result of your interaction together.

make time for plain old fun

My husband and I have figured out a great way to get together with friends without having to hire a babysitter. As soon as our kids' (early) bedtime routines are completed, I drive over to my friend Em's house where her one-year-old is in bed, and Em's husband drives straight to our house where my husband is monitoring our snoozing kids. This reciprocal arrangement allows both my husband and I to get some needed interaction with a friend. Our latest tradeoff was the highlight of my week. While the guys ate Italian appetizers and watched *The Godfather*, Em and I scrapbooked, ate cookies and popcorn, and just talked—without interruptions! There wasn't anything overtly spiritual in our get-together, but I believe God was pleased. God is the Creator of friendship, and times like that—simple, fun, and bonding—are blessings from him.

My friend Kelly, who is a bit of a domestic diva, holds a monthly event at her house she calls Sew Fun Night. It started when she began teaching a few of her friends how to sew simple quilts. Now she'll host as many as fifteen women in her home on a given night, most of them working on some sort of craft (like designing greeting cards, knitting, or scrapbooking) and some who absolutely hate crafts and are there just to enjoy the fun. There is no agenda for the evening other than conversation and getting away from the hectic pace of life. With husbands or babysitters watching the kids at home, this once-a-month escape is a breath of fresh air for the busy moms who come.

Your to-do list may be crammed, but here's one more thing to add: plain old fun! Time spent enjoying life with friends is refreshing and refocusing; it helps us step back from problems or frustrations that can plague us and allows us to just be ourselves. Also, having fun allows stress, hurts, and worries to be healed through God's gift of laughter and smiling. You can meet a friend for lunch or even just plan on a fifteen-minute coffee break together during a tough day at work. Fun with friends doesn't have to be kid free; you can all have fun together by meeting up for picnics, going on walks, gathering the kids to make cookies together, or meeting at the mall food court. As your kids watch you interact with other moms, you're helping them develop a healthy perspective on the important role of friendship in a Christian's life.

enlist a soul helper

150

Sometimes we can't see the forest for the trees when it comes to our faith. We may have doubts, wrestle with discouraging questions, or feel directionless and confused. As busy moms who may not see even the *trees* because we're so busy wiping noses, we desperately need another perspective. We need someone in our lives who *can* see the forest—and can help us step back and see it too. This type of intimate fellowship—in which another Christ follower walks with you on your journey with Jesus—can take several different forms, such as mentoring, accountability partnering, or spiritual direction.

> [T]he Christian needs another Christian who speaks God's Word to him…[H]is own heart is uncertain, his brother's is sure.
>
> —Dietrich Bonhoeffer

Mentoring. In a mentoring relationship, a more mature (and usually older) Christian meets with another believer and aids her by partnering in prayer and Bible study, by suggesting spiritual growth practices, and by giving advice or pastoral care regarding life situations. In the context of this type of relationship, we can practice another important spiritual discipline: submission (also called obedience). We live in a society that worships independence and self-sufficiency, but in practicing submission we willfully place ourselves under the authority and guidance of another. We invite our mentor to challenge us to grow in certain ways or to suggest specific avenues of life application, and then we follow through. In essence, we submit to and obey God by following the direction he provides us through another person.

Accountability Partnering. Accountability relationships usually take place between spiritual peers who commit to speak candidly with each other about sin patterns and struggles in their lives, promising to confess openly to one another. As Dietrich Bonhoeffer wrote, it is in this willing vulnerability and "confession [that] the break-through to community takes place. . . . The more isolated a person is, the more destructive will be the power of sin over him. . . . In confession the light of the Gospel breaks into the darkness and seclusion of the heart."[1] As accountability partners grapple with tough sins and extend God's grace and forgiveness to each other, they're able to work together, through prayer and biblical encouragement, to help one another battle temptations and keep their spiritual commitments.

Spiritual Direction. A form of spiritual help less commonly practiced in evangelical churches than mentoring or accountability is spiritual direction. Yet it is an important and vital avenue for Christian growth. In a spiritual direction relationship, "help [is] given by one Christian to another which enables that person to pay attention to God's personal communication to him or her, to respond to this personally communicating God, and to live out the consequences of the relationship."[2] Spiritual direction relationships are different than accountability or mentoring relationships in their focus. Rather than talking about life problems, providing pastoral care or counsel, or discussing theological issues, a spiritual director's "conversation" is made up mostly of quietness, prayer, and attention to the Holy Spirit with only occasional speaking. Through asking questions and helping the directee listen to God and see how God has been speaking to her, a spiritual director keeps the focus "on the relationship itself between God and person. The person is helped not so much to *understand* that relationship better, but to *engage* in it, to enter into dialogue with God. Spiritual direction . . . focuses on what happens when a person listens to and responds to a self-communicating God."[3]

> [A]lthough the Holy Spirit is our ultimate Guide, God has chosen to use fellow believers as instruments of growth. God could work holiness in our lives by the direct application of His sheer power. But His customary way of working good is through other believers.
>
> —Bruce Demarest

God may be calling you to jump into a committed mentoring relationship or to add an element of accountability to an existing friendship. Or perhaps God may prompt you to meet with an older Christian for spiritual direction on either an as-needed or a committed basis. Do you have a soul helper? If not, ask God to show you who he wants to use to speak into your life.

look outside your network

Contrary to popular belief and common practice, God's intention for authentic fellowship is not that we should surround ourselves with clones—people just like us, who are just our age, have our same tastes, think like us, vote like us, and generally always agree with us. Though it's true that our very best friends will usually be people who have a lot in common with us, we miss out on the richness of God's family if we only fellowship with like-minded people in our same stage of life.

Remember my friend Amie who had just moved to a new city? That wasn't the first time she's had to pull up roots and relocate: she's moved six times in the last seven years! Along the way, God has taught her some amazing truths about fellowship: most important that true fellowship can be found in surprising places. She remembers the day that lesson was learned at an inner-city African-American church she and her husband attended:

> We would usually arrive at church early on Sundays, before Bible study, and Mr. Lewis would be there. He was in his seventies, quiet, and seemed to carry a certain calm with him. It took me awhile even to notice Mr. Lewis. He sat on a chair just outside the sanctuary. I was reluctant to talk to him at first. What could we talk about? What could we possibly have in common? But as we began to talk, I realized that the gulf between us wasn't really that wide. We were both questioners who were not content to take things at face value. I came to appreciate his quiet spirit and his determination in the face of painful obstacles as he recovered from knee surgery. I learned about his family, and he learned about mine. Each week I began to respect and appreciate him even more.
>
> We didn't become best friends or anything. We didn't plan trips together to the mall. But at a time in my life when God knew that I needed that connection and also the push to look outside my comfort zone, he provided a listening ear and some words of wisdom and encouragement from an unlikely place.

We often meet God when we step outside of our comfort zone; fellowship is no exception to that rule. Fellowship isn't just a matter of being with people who make us feel at ease—it can also be personally challenging, causing us to question assumptions, opening our eyes and ears to different viewpoints, and enabling us to step into another's shoes.

Who may be a Mr. Lewis in your life? If you open your heart to God's leading and commit to willingly step outside your existing relationships, you may be surprised at the wonderful and rich things God

the four circles of fellowship		
principle	**biblical models**	**examples**
the large circle	We are members of the global church, united with Christians all around the planet. God also intends us to fellowship in our local churches, joining in with the family of believers nearby.	• The early church (Acts 2:42–47) • The body of Christ (1 Cor. 12:12–20)	• Attendance at church services • Membership in a local church body • Participation in large Christian events • Receiving the Lord's Supper with your local congregation • Praying for or getting to know Christians in other countries or from other cultures
the small circle	We can get to know others better in the context of smaller group interaction. In small-circle fellowship, we regularly participate in gatherings of approximately four to twenty believers.	• Jesus' twelve disciples (Luke 6:13–16) • Jesus' close friendship with Lazarus, Mary, and Martha (Luke 10:38–42; John 11:1–45)	• Getting involved in an adult Sunday school class • Being part of a small group Bible study • Joining a mom's group or a Christian play-date group
the inner circle	For sharing the private details of our lives, we need intimate, one-to-one interactions in which we feel safe and can choose to be vulnerable.	• David and Jonathan (1 Sam. 18:1–3) • Ruth and Naomi (Ruth 1:1–19) • Paul and Timothy (1 Tim. 1:2, 18; 2 Tim. 1:2)	• Having a close personal friendship • Meeting with a mentor • Committing to an accountability partnership • Participating in spiritual direction
the family circle	We don't always need to look outside our everyday life for fellowship. God has built fellowship right into our lives through our closest relationships with other Christ-followers: our husbands, parents or in-laws, siblings, and even children.	• Lois, Eunice, and Timothy (2 Tim. 1:5)	• Having family devotions • Praying with your spouse • Sharing Scriptures and encouragement with relatives

has to teach you through the diverse life experiences of another person. You may never feel led to become best friends with that person—but real, enriching fellowship can happen even in brief encounters.

include four circles of fellowship

Whether we're social butterflies or wallflowers, outspoken extroverts who thrive in large groups or soft-spoken introverts who have just one or two friends, God designed *all* of us to grow best by experiencing multiple levels of fellowship. Take a moment to read through the chart on page 154.

Do you feel a longing for more fellowship in your life? Using these four circles, take a fellowship inventory of your life. Which type of fellowship are you most hungry for? Are you involved in each of these types of fellowship in some way? If not, is there one circle of fellowship you can focus on developing in your life? How do you feel God may be calling you to grow and stretch yourself when it comes to the discipline of fellowship?

There will be seasons of motherhood during which it is impossible to participate in all four circles of fellowship—when we're caring for a newborn and functioning on three hours of sleep, when our child cries hysterically every time he's dropped off at the church nursery, when our children are constantly passing around illnesses to each other. And that's OK—practicing fellowship isn't about *accomplishing* something. In fact, it is during times like this that we can really benefit from true fellowship by relying on other Christians to help us: to pray for us, provide meals, or give us a call to check in on us. But by keeping these four circles in mind, we can maintain a healthy perspective on how God designed us to grow best relationally, emotionally, and spiritually.

it ain't easy

Practicing fellowship can be a huge blessing in our lives, helping us feel encouraged, uplifted, understood, healed, and cared for. At other times the experience of fellowship may be best summarized by a humorously titled magazine article I saw once: "How Will I Be Able to *Stand* Heaven With All Those Annoying People There?!" Practicing fellowship can be hard work—that's when we get a true sense of why it is a spiritual *discipline*. It requires effort and commitment to show love and caring to a Christian brother or sister who gets on your nerves. It takes grit and guts to get to know someone who is different from you. It requires courage and personal risk to really open up and be vulnerable with another believer. It takes hard-nosed determination combined with lots of grace to forgive a Christian who's wronged or wounded you. It requires intense trust in God to confess specific sins to another flawed sinner. It takes effort to put our independent spirit aside and submit to the spiritual guidance of a mentor.

But fellowship can and does happen because of this one factor: Christ in us. "If we walk in the light, as he is in the light, we have fellowship with one another" (1 John 1:7). When we walk in Christ—when we follow his example and strive to live as his disciples—we're enabled to have true fellowship, even when it's hard. Bonhoeffer summed it up perfectly when he wrote, "Whether it be a brief, single encounter or the daily fellowship of years, Christian community is only this. We belong to one another only through and in Jesus Christ."[4]

talk about it

Discuss these questions with a friend or a small group of other moms.

1. Describe a typical conversation you have with others at church on a Sunday morning. Does it get as honest and real as you'd like it to? Why or why not?

2. What do you think are the most common barriers to true fellowship for most Christians? What are some barriers specific to moms?

3. Describe a recent fun time you had with a friend. What did you enjoy about it? What were the spiritual benefits that resulted from having some plain old fun?

157

4. When has someone functioned as a soul helper in your life (whether that person knew it or not)? How did God use him or her to impact your faith?

5. In which circle of fellowship do you most desire to grow? What ideas do you have for participating in that type of fellowship?

try it

Here are ten ideas you can try.

1. Read these passages about fellowship: Proverbs 27:17; John 17:6–23; Romans 12:3–5, 15:5–6; Ephesians 4:2–6; Colossians 3:12–15; and James 5:16. How would you define fellowship based on what you've read? Journal your thoughts.

2. Plan a fun get together with a friend, such as the babysitting swap described on page 149 or a lunch date (with kids along for the ride). Just enjoy your friend's company—kick back, laugh, smile, and celebrate God's gift of friendship.

3. Send an encouraging e-mail to someone who might *need* fellowship—someone who's overbusy, lonely, burned out, or stressed.

4. Write down the name of someone from your church family who is different from you but whom you believe God wants you to connect with: _____.
The next time you see that person, take some time to get to know him or her, and be sure to get beyond surfacy small talk.

5. Journal your response to these questions: How has fellowship enabled you to implement other spiritual disciplines in your life? Or how has a lack of fellowship hindered your efforts to grow? What role do you want fellowship to have in your future spiritual growth?

6. Set aside an evening to focus on family-circle fellowship by talking about Scripture with your husband, doing a Bible craft with your kids, or singing worship songs together as a family.

7. Use a Bible computer program or Web site (such as www.biblegateway.com) to look up and read all the uses of the phrase "one another" in the New Testament. You'll be inspired and convicted by God's high standard for how we are to interact with and relate to other Christians!

8. If you are struggling with a private sin or a pattern of spiritual weakness that you've kept to yourself, decide *right now* that you'll confess it to a mature Christian. Ask God for help—he will give you the courage.

9. Memorize Psalm 133:1. Whenever another Christian gets on your nerves, repeat this verse to yourself and ask God to help you work for unity.

10. Talk to your pastor, women's ministry coordinator, or another church leader about helping you connect with a soul helper who can mentor you, provide spiritual direction, or come alongside you as an accountability partner.

11

worship and celebration

The scene is universal: You can observe the same reaction in a hut in Botswana, a hospital in Moscow, or a farmhouse in rural Montana. It's the teary-eyed look of utter, complete, raw joy when a mother is handed her newborn baby for the very first time. What a miracle! What a gift! What a reason to celebrate!

From that first moment on, motherhood—in spite of its trials and heartaches—is jam-packed with causes for celebration. Can you relate to the feelings of these moms?

Pastor's Wife and Mom of Three: "When I held my newborn children, I had a brand-new feeling—a complete awe of our amazing Creator and how intricate and perfect all his designs are!"

Part-Time Working Mom of Three: "Becoming a mom gave me a totally new understanding of how God loved me. I see my relationship with my child and how much I love this helpless being who thinks he knows everything but really knows nothing. In my relationship with God, I now understand how little I really know and how much God loves me in spite of the fact that I think I know everything."

Mom of Three Preschoolers: "God has shown me how seeing the world through the eyes of a child is much more refreshing than the ruts I fall into in how I view things. It's so much fun to share their excitement and enthusiasm over little things like bugs and snow and wind and ice cream!"

> Every good and perfect gift is from above.
>
> —James 1:17

Your children (and every other good thing in your life) are amazing gifts from God. God has given us myriads of reasons to celebrate and worship him: spring tulips, laughter with friends, brilliant constellations, little hands holding ours, quiet sunsets, words of love, woolly bear caterpillars, snow angels. And beyond these gifts are the great spiritual blessings from God: Jesus' sacrifice on the cross, his victorious resurrection, his offer of forgiveness and salvation, the Holy Spirit's presence in our lives. With all these reasons to worship, it seems strange to call celebration and worship spiritual disciplines. Shouldn't they be natural outpourings of our delight in God?

Well, yes, they *should*. But living in a constant mind-set of worship and celebration doesn't always come naturally. In fact, in those motherhood moments of frustration, worship is often the last thing on our minds.

never too much

The word *worship* essentially means "worth-ship"—declaring the worth or value of something. In worship, we focus on and declare eternal, unchanging truths about who God is. And when we're talking about God's worth and his awesome and amazing qualities, there should be no limit to our worship!

Writer Donald S. Whitney explained worship this way: "Worship is the God-centered focus and response of the inner man; it is being preoccupied with God. . . . [W]henever you do focus on the infinite worth of God, you will respond in worship as surely as the moon reflects the sun."[1] And it's true: Worship is an instinctive response to our awareness of who God is. Our struggle with the spiritual discipline of worship as busy moms with hectic lives usually isn't a result of doubt. We don't question God's worthiness of worship—we're simply so distracted and preoccupied with other things that we aren't able to adequately focus on God in our inner being; other, more "urgent" issues push thoughts of God to the side.

> Praise should be proportionate to its object; therefore let it be infinite when rendered unto the Lord. We cannot praise Him too much, too often, too zealously, too carefully, too joyfully.
>
> —Charles Haddon Spurgeon

Closely tied to worship, the discipline of celebration is focusing on and delight in what God does. We are celebrating when we take joy in our children, in flowers, in music, in friendship. We're celebrating when we express thanks for good food, for God's provision, for sunrises, and for faith. The spiritual discipline of celebration is, in essence, when "We concentrate on *our* life and world as God's work and as God's gift to us."[2]

The real challenge in practicing celebration comes when life doesn't seem to be going so well—when financial trouble, sickness, or plain old stress gets us down. These are the times when life doesn't feel carefree and joyous; instead it feels lonely, oppressive, melancholy. These are the times when it seems like James may have been a bit crazy for writing, "Consider it pure joy, my brothers and sisters, whenever you face trials of many kinds" (James 1:2 TNIV). Yet it is in these moments when our faith in God and our trust that he will buoy us through the storm sets us apart from the world. As Richard Foster explained, "Freedom from anxiety and care forms the basis for celebration. Because we know he cares for us, we can cast all our care upon him. . . . When we trust God we are free to rely entirely upon him to provide what we need. The decision to set the mind on higher things is an act of the will. That is why celebration is a Discipline."[3]

putting it into action: mom-friendly ideas

Celebrating and trusting God when we're caught up in a whirlwind of negative emotions takes grit and effort. And turning our minds toward worshiping God in the middle of a crazy day takes determination and persistence. These "easy" and "natural" disciplines can sometimes be a spiritual workout! Yet even when they require spiritual sweat, practicing the disciplines of worship and celebration is a must for moms. When we delight in God and in his work, we model for our children a proper and true perspective of the world—and we find refreshment for our own thirsty souls.

attend church

There's something strange about pregnancy hormones: Nearly every Sunday morning during both of my pregnancies, when I stood and joined the congregation in singing worship songs or hymns, I'd get choked up. I don't mean this figuratively—I literally had to stop singing because my throat would constrict in a near convulsion as tears pooled in my eyes. It wasn't an allergic reaction to the music— it's just that, for some reason, it all seemed incredibly beautiful. So each Sunday I nearly had to run out of the service bawling because of the spiritual awe I felt at being a part of a ragtag group of believers, belting out our praises to God together. This is what God made us for! This is what we'll be doing forever in heaven!

And even without the estrogen boost of pregnancy, we all can experience the beauty of worshiping God with others. Look at this compelling portrait of fellowship in Ephesians: "Speak to one another with psalms, hymns and spiritual songs. Sing and make music in your heart to the Lord, always giving thanks to God the Father for everything, in the name of our Lord Jesus Christ" (5:19–20). God designed us to worship with one another. When we joyfully participate in a church service—singing together, hearing and speaking Scripture to each other, participating in the Lord's Supper together—we get a glimpse of our unity as a body, as God's Church. And we do together what God created his Church to do: declare his glory.

163

If you regularly attend church, then you're likely already participating in corporate worship and celebration. But there's more to it than just showing up; only you know the focus of your heart during a church service. Next Sunday, ask God to help you focus on him in your inner being so you can respond in glowing worship just as "the moon reflects the sun." And if you don't belong to a church, then find one and dive right in! No church is perfect, and you don't have to be perfect to be part of one.

praise along with your kids.

"Glow-oh-oh-oh-oh-ohhh-ria! In a great big eggshell!" These are the "lyrics" my three-year-old still recites after hearing "Angels We Have Heard On High" sung at our church last Christmas, more than five months ago. I'm not sure how he latched on to that carol, but he still sings it almost daily, belting it out especially loudly when we go on walks around the neighborhood. It's cute, but it's also praise. Although his interpretation of *in excelsis deo* doesn't make logical sense to any person listening, it makes perfect sense to one Person: God. Nonsense praise songs and newborn cries are hymns of praise to our Maker. The psalmist recognized this truth when he wrote, "You have set your glory above the heavens. From the lips of children and infants you have ordained praise" (Ps. 8:1–2).

Jesus powerfully repeated these same words to the Pharisees who were indignant on Palm Sunday when little kids were shouting forth the great truth of the universe, "Hosanna to the Son of David" (Matt. 21:15). This is the Messiah! This is the Christ! Just like the children on that triumphant day, God has created your kids with a cosmos-shaking purpose: to declare God's praise! And kids instinctively know how to do this—they are uninhibited in their dancing, unself-conscious in their smiles, undeterred in their fits of laughter. You can join them in their delight and celebration of God.

There are countless creative ways you can worship and celebrate God with your kids. Here are just a few ideas:

- Get a kid-friendly worship CD and let your kids pick songs they want to sing. Then belt them out together in the car or family room.

- Do a craft together that celebrates truths about God.

- Make a fruit salad together, inviting your children to share one quality that they love about God for each type of fruit they add to the bowl.

- Sing a worship song as a prayer each night at bedtime.

- Go on a praise hunt during a day at the park by challenging kids to find an example of a way something in nature was praising God (such as a flower blooming, a bird singing, or a butterfly taking flight).

- Make up songs together based on worshipful Scripture passages.

- Create a family gratitude calendar by listing something you're thankful for each day. Then throw a party at the end of the month to recount and celebrate all God did.

- Sing hymns together as a family before dinner each night, helping your kids gain familiarity with some of the amazing lyrics that proclaim truths about God.

- Hand out instruments (or make them, such as "shakers" made out of toilet paper rolls and dried beans) and invite everyone to make a joyful noise unto the Lord!

- Help your kids make their own books of worship by drawing a picture to worship God each day, then stapling them together.

- Celebrate things God has done for you using the alphabet, naming one item of celebration for each letter.

165

Try to set aside time for worship every day with your kids; whether it's five minutes of singing in the car or a gooey-fingered glue-stick craft, these moments will be precious to you—and to God.

celebrate with family and friends

In *The Life You've Always Wanted*, John Ortberg explained that the importance of celebration "is a primary reason we see much emphasis placed on feast days in the Old Testament. Times of feasting were to be transforming experiences—just as times of meditating or fasting were. Celebration generally involves activities that bring pleasure—gathering with people we love, eating and drinking, singing and dancing."[4] And just as the Old Testament prescribes special fast and feast days throughout the Jewish calendar year, so the Christian Church calendar can similarly guide us through experiences of fasting, feasting, celebrating, and worshiping together. Some Christian traditions structure their entire ministry around the Church calendar; my church background, on the other hand, focused mostly on celebrating Christmas and Easter. Yet over the past few years, my husband, David, and I have read and thought more about how our family can develop family traditions that keep our hearts focused on the rhythms of God's story throughout the entire year, including Advent, Epiphany, Lent, Holy Week, and Pentecost, along with our celebrations of Christmas morning and Easter Sunday. These have been special times of fasting and feasting — of declaring who God is and delighting in his good gifts. In fact, right now our kitchen sink is piled high with dishes from one such feast; last night eight adults and six kids joined us for a messianic Passover seder — a meal marking Maundy Thursday, the night Jesus celebrated the Last Supper with his disciples. The event was filled with moments of prayer and spiritual reflection along with the realities of family life: sending kids to time out, noisy play by two- and three-year-olds, some serious spills of the sparkling grape juice, and two three-year-olds putting a poor two-year-old "in jail" against his will! It was exhausting and it made a huge mess, but it was fun *and* God was present.

What can your family do to begin some of your own traditions of celebration together? These may be structured around the Church calendar, they may be drawn from your own family background, or they may be your own brand-new creative ideas. You could

- Commit to fast from something as a family during Lent.
- Pray a special blessing over your child as part of his or her birthday party.
- Celebrate the four Sundays of Advent by lighting candles and talking about the story of Christ's coming into the world.
- Invite some friends (with kids) over for a New Year's Eve pizza party and ask everyone to share something awesome about God.

- Sing a traditional Easter hymn together every Easter Sunday.

- Have an annual family campout and spend a night stargazing, talking together about God's eternal qualities.

These are just a few ideas—I'm sure you can come up with plenty of your own. The point isn't to do something elaborate; it is to intentionally weave the celebration of God's blessings into the rhythm of your family's life.

167

rediscover the sabbath

One of my childhood playmates was a neighbor named Christy. On sunny Sunday afternoons, I'd usually wander over to her house to see if she could come out and play. The answer was always the same: With a rather depressed and embarrassed look on her face, Christy would tell me week after week that no, she couldn't play. It was the Sabbath. It was "family day." I must have been a little blockheaded because it took me years to get the idea that this was a hard-and-fast family rule. Christy could never play with me on a Sunday, no matter how persistently I showed up at her front door.

Some families like Christy's keep the Sabbath with absolute rigidity, forbidding any activity but staying indoors and resting. That may seem a bit extreme to many of us; yet if we are totally honest we'll likely admit that we don't keep the Sabbath at all. It seems impractical, unnecessary, outdated. After all, wouldn't it cause more stress to set aside a day to rest than to take advantage of the opportunity to get things done?

But the Sabbath is God's gift to us. Through this weekly holiday, we realign our ordinary, distracted week with the extraordinary reality of our Creator and his act of creation. Rediscovering the

Sabbath and deciding how you and your family might practice it can become one of the most significant patterns of worship and celebration in your family's life. In her inspiring book *Receiving the Day*, Christian historian (and mother of twins) Dorothy Bass explored what the Sabbath and God's gift of time can mean in growing and stretching our faith. She explained, "When we keep a Sabbath holy, we are practicing, for a day, the freedom that God intends for all people. . . . We are trying on a new way of life as we begin to allow our weeks to be changed in response to God's promises. . . . Like a novice learning to play a musical instrument, we may be off-key at times. It may be years before we are in harmony, and we will never get it perfect. But that need not stop us. Besides, stopping is less a problem than getting started."[5] So how do you get started in practicing the Sabbath? In addition to resting from work, Bass suggested that families consider celebrating the Sabbath by resting from commerce and worry, instead spending time worshiping God, enjoying and caring for creation, visiting with friends, and making memories as a family.

If keeping the Sabbath is a practice of celebration and worship, then rigid legalism has no place in it. This isn't a matter of creating a list of don'ts for a day, thus torturing your kids (and yourself) by confining everyone to loneliness and boredom. It is an opportunity to intentionally live differently and to embrace a Christian pattern for your family's week. What can remembering the Sabbath mean for you and your family? What can you do to set one day aside — to make it special, celebratory, freeing? Seek God's guidance; he will delight in your efforts to delight in him.

get alone with god

As a kid, I had a bit of a crush on Moses (a.k.a. Charlton Heston). One of my favorite parts of *The Ten Commandments* movie was when Moses saw the burning bush and then heard God's deep, booming voice telling him to take off his sandals because he was standing on holy ground. Wow! How amazing it would be to actually hear God's voice! (I think the other reason I really liked the scene is that it was the last time Moses looked good— after meeting God, he suddenly turned old and gray!)

Worshiping God with your immediate family and your church family is important, but practicing the discipline of worship must also include times when you worship God individually. Like Moses on holy ground, we need some sandals-off moments—times when it's just us and the Lord, when there aren't a million distractions, when we put aside our to-do lists and focus on who God is.

169

For moms this can be a real challenge because time alone is such a rarity. But as with some other disciplines we've discussed so far, there are ways to repurpose those few moments alone and preoccupy our hearts with God. Getting up twenty minutes early to have some time alone with God, using our children's quiet times or nap times to celebrate God's gifts, or worshiping God when we're alone in the car are all great options. And when we can't find time to actually be alone, we could always just throw an apron over our heads.

What?!

It's not as far-fetched as it sounds. Susanna Wesley, the mother of famed preacher John Wesley; his hymn-writing brother, Charles; and eight other surviving children, quite literally never had a moment alone. Yet she was able to have sandals-off moments on a daily basis—time when she could meet "alone" with God. Her method was simple: She pulled her apron up over her face to pray and speak to God. The apron on her head was a signal to her kids: Don't bother mom right now, or you'll be in big trouble!

I can see her in my mind's eye, breathing quietly under the fabric, imagining for a moment that she isn't surrounded by chaos and the demands of motherhood. Maybe she even pictured herself kneeling in God's presence. Perhaps she was able to still the sounds around her and just hear quietness or hum a worshipful tune. The essence of what went on under that apron is between her and God, but her example is compelling to us even today. Though we may not feel comfortable literally covering our heads and ignoring our kids for a short time, we can find some way to be alone and worship God.

When you're alone with God, there are many ways you can worship him and celebrate what he is doing in your life. You can sing hymns or songs, you can speak words of praise from the psalms, you can silently meditate on God's awesome qualities, or you can write a letter of love and thanks to him. Or, if you're in the middle of a trying time when celebration just isn't coming naturally, you can try keeping a thanksgiving journal, writing at least one thing you are grateful for each day. Even in our darkest moments, we have much to thank God for, and the practice of writing these things down can often help pull us through the darkness into the light of joy.

> Worship will turn our values, habits, and ideas upside-down as it forms our character; only then will we be genuinely right-side up eternally. Only then will we know a Joy worthy of our destiny.
>
> —Marva J. Dawn

your spiritual act of worship

As mothers, we have so much to be thankful for that words may be insufficient to express our gratitude. When we reflect on the gifts of our children, our families, our friends, and when we consider the ultimate gift of salvation, we simply *must* respond in worship and celebration. Beyond music, spoken words, or the arts, the greatest way to practice the disciplines of worship and celebration is to live a holy life through the power of God's Spirit. Psalm

29:2 (KJV) tells us to "worship the LORD in the beauty of holiness." The Apostle Paul went further when he referred specifically to God-honoring living and thinking: "I urge you, brothers, in view of God's mercy, to offer your bodies as living sacrifices, holy and pleasing to God—this is your spiritual act of worship. Do not conform any longer to the pattern of this world, but be transformed by the renewing of your mind" (Rom. 12:1–2).

When we seek to live as Jesus' followers by practicing the spiritual disciplines in our daily lives, *we are worshiping*. When we attend to God with a silent heart, when we seek his voice through meditating on his Word, when we ask his help in effecting life change, when we demonstrate love by serving another person, when we adjust our budget to live as better stewards, *we are worshiping*. In each of the spiritual disciplines we offer ourselves to God, presenting our physical actions, our wills, and our thoughts as sacrifices of praise to him. This is the beauty we offer to God: our desire and effort, with the Spirit's life-changing power, to live a life that is holy and pleasing to our perfect, good, and loving maker. As Harold M. Best put it in *Unceasing Worship*,

> The beauty of holiness for a continuing worshiper is nothing less than purity of heart, manifest in working out our salvation while knowing that God-through-Christ is in us, working both to will and to do his good pleasure. . . . It is, in essence, being like Christ. . . . There is nothing more real than to be in Christ and to live in Christ—to walk, run, hunger, thirst, press on, work out our salvation and be living epistles.[6]

talk about it

Discuss these questions with a friend or a small group of other moms.

1. When you think about your life as a mom, what reasons do you see to worship and celebrate? Share a few examples.

2. When have the disciplines of worship and celebration come naturally to you? When have worshiping or celebrating been difficult or felt impossible? Explain.

3. Do you think worship and celebration are essential to the Christian life? Why or why not?

4. Describe a meaningful experience you've had worshiping God or celebrating his works either alone, with your family, or with other Christians.

5. How do you want to include more practices of worship and celebration in your life? What ideas do you have that you can share with other moms?

try it

Here are ten ideas you can try.

1. Read these passages that celebrate and worship God: Job 19:23–27; Psalm 9:1–2, 100:1–5, 136:1–26; James 1:17; and Revelation 4:8–11. How does your heart respond when you read them? What do *you* want to say to God? Journal your thoughts.

2. When you sit down at church next Sunday, quietly ask God to "preoccupy" your heart with him and keep your focus on worship. When distracting thoughts pop into your head,

acknowledge them and give them to God. Then refocus your heart on worship and celebration.

3. Flip through pictures of your children's first few weeks of life. As you do, thank God for the blessing of your children.

4. Meditate on the words of the hymn "How Great Thou Art."

5. Celebrate by beginning a new family tradition! See page 166 for ideas.

6. Schedule a half hour this week when you can be alone, whether it is early in the morning, late at night, or when a babysitter can swing by. Spend that time alone with God, focused entirely on worshiping him.

7. Plan a kid-friendly worship experience for your family each day this week. See page 164 for ideas.

8. Read about the many different ways people can worship God by exploring the worshipful acts and words of Bezalel (Exod. 31), David (the Psalms), Jesus' mother, Mary (Luke 1:46–55), Mary of Bethany (John 12:1–8), and Thomas (John 20:28). Journal about the various avenues of worship and identify the types of worship you most enjoy offering God.

9. Make this Sunday a true Sabbath by treating the day differently from the rest of the week.

10. Commit to keep a thanksgiving journal for at least one month, writing about one thing you're thankful for every day. Review your journal on a weekly basis.

12

real moms,
real faith,
real change

Y ou've made it! Somehow, between bedtime routines and diaper changing, long hours at work or late nights of laundry, kissing stubbed toes and coaxing sneezes out of little noses, microwaving leftovers and scrubbing crayon off the wall, you found time to journey all the way through this book. God has taken you on an adventure through fifteen spiritual disciplines drawn from the rich history of his Church; you've sampled a taste of silence, solitude, scriptural learning, prayer, meditation, life change, service, evangelism, hospitality, simplicity, stewardship, fasting, fellowship, worship, and celebration. And along the way, God has done some renovation in your life: refreshing you, reviving you, stretching you, connecting with your heart in new and unexpected ways. And he's not finished—the renovation process has just begun!

The disciplines you've explored—the Christian practices for training, striving, and growing in faith—are tools Jesus wants to use in your life to make you more like him. As you've explored the practices in this book, no doubt God has already been speaking to you, nudging you toward certain disciplines and practices and convicting you of your need to make some specific changes in your life. As you come to the end of this book, don't just close the cover and move on; take some time to create a blueprint for the renovation process God has begun in your life. Reflect on where he's led you so far and consider where he wants you to go.

blueprinting growth   175

There are many avenues for discovering where God wants you to go from here; here are three that I've found particularly helpful on my own spiritual journey.

create a training plan

Recently, I caught up with Anna, an old friend from my college years. I remembered her as a vibrant, bubbly, enthusiastic Christian with a great sense of humor. Back then, Anna had many interests, but athletics was definitely *not* one of them. I never knew her to work out or show even remote interest in exercise. So when I reconnected with her, I was delighted to see her kind smile but, to be honest, was totally surprised at her trim physique. It turned out that in the years since we'd last spoken, Anna had become a runner.

"How did you do it?" I asked, in total amazement and admiration.

"Not to sound cheesy," she said, "but I have to quote Nike: You *just do it.*"

Then Anna explained how, after firmly deciding to pursue running, she consulted a friend who was a marathoner and got on a training plan. This plan was really for beginners: The first couple of weeks involved about one minute of jogging and only ten minutes of walking per day! But eventually, by consistently training, she accomplished her goal. A bona fide runner, she now regularly participates in marathons.

The key was that Anna didn't just decide one day to "give it a try" and run a marathon. Just trying—even trying hard—would've led to failure, discouragement, and pain. She needed a plan that would take her from where she was to where she wanted to be. The same principle is true when it comes to spiritual growth. Check out the words of pastor and writer John Ortberg: "For much of my life, when I heard messages about following Jesus, I thought in terms of *trying hard* to be like him. . . . Spiritual transformation is not a matter of trying harder, but of *training wisely*."[1] Practicing spiritual disciplines isn't about trying—it's a way of training (gumnazo) to be more like Christ.

176

Now that you've finished this book and you're wondering "Where do I go from here?" it's a great time to come up with a training plan. Keep in mind Rule 2 (see page 21 for a refresher): You're not allowed to identify thirty-seven ways in which you need to grow! Instead, prayerfully ask God to help you focus on one or two areas to zero in on. God may lead you to dive deeper into a new discipline you experienced and enjoyed as you journeyed through this book. Or God may prompt you to give a weak area of your life a workout by training yourself with a "tough" discipline—one you didn't like as much when you sampled it the first time. Or perhaps God may want you to explore all the disciplines again by concentrating on one for a month or two and then moving on to another one. Use My Training Plan on page 180 to help you think it through and map out a few specific steps you'll take to implement spiritual change. Then pray, thanking God for his leading in your life and relying on his help as you train (gumnazo) and strive (askeo) to be more and more like Jesus.

seek counsel and support

When it comes to a routine for physical training, we're much more likely to stick with it when we have a coach, a trainer, or an exercise partner. The same is true of our spiritual training. Don't try to grow all alone! Whether you get plugged in to an intense mentoring relationship or you simply want to keep a Christian friend posted about your goals and your progress or struggles, the help and support of someone alongside you will strengthen you during the tough times.

keep a journal

If you've been following the Try It suggestion to journal your reflections about each discipline, then you've already discovered the value of journaling. Rereading a journal is like traveling through time. It's an opportunity to step back to an earlier stage in your spiritual growth with the advantage of hindsight; you're able to see God's leading, sense God's plan unfolding, and celebrate his continuous presence in your life. Whether you're an avid writer who could journal for hours daily, or you instead fit in five minutes of writing every few days, keeping a journal that reflects on your spiritual experiences and your daily life is a practice God can use to speak to you in powerful ways. It is a way of being in the present with God, sharing your honest thoughts and feelings, exploring questions and doubts, and seeking God's direction. Journaling can be a great avenue for practicing

177

- *Prayer.* For some people, writing down prayers is a method that helps them stay focused.

- *Scripture Meditation.* You can write out meaningful Scripture passages, note your thoughts and feelings, and explore what you feel God is saying to you.

- *Examen.* A journal is a great tool for taking stock of your spiritual life, attitudes, thoughts, and behaviors at the end of a day.

- *Worship and Celebration.* Exercises like writing poems or praise, penning song lyrics, or keeping a thanksgiving journal can help you keep a celebration perspective even during tough times.

* *Spiritual Self-Discovery.* A journal can become a moving record of God's love weaving through your life. Consider journaling about memories and thoughts prompted by questions like these: When in my life have I most longed for God? How has God led me through challenging situations? Who have been the most significant spiritual influences in my life? How have I specifically needed and experienced God's forgiveness? When have been the most vibrant seasons of my spiritual life? Which aspects of my spiritual life have been neglected in the past? What dreams has God given me for my life?

If taking a pen to a blank book intimidates you, you might want to try typing a journal on the computer; the words will start flowing if you just consider it a collection of brief e-mails to God. Or you could keep an audio journal by using a handheld tape recorder to speak your thoughts.

When you journal, think of it as a private conversation; you don't have to impress anybody with what you say. Instead, consider it a brief retreat from others around you—your chance to just be the real you.

embracing the high calling of motherhood

Being a mom isn't easy, and it's natural during those most stressful days to wistfully remember what life was like B.C. (Before Children). My thoughts go something like this: *Oh, the hours and hours I had to worship and pray! The time I had to sleep in or soak in the tub! The meaningful conversations with friends; my ability to focus, undistracted, during sermons; the long early mornings of profound and insightful Bible study . . . and so on, and* so on, and so on. During those moments, I wear some seriously rose-colored glasses!

Yes, spiritual growth was easier in some ways before the tremendous responsibilities of parenting came into our lives—but easier isn't necessarily better. If we're going to be honest, we have to admit that we're usually not realistic about what we actually did in the B.C. years. And second, we're missing out on the tremendous blessing God intends for us to discover in the challenges, trials, and stretching moments of parenthood. We aren't meant to escape from parenthood in order to grow spiritually—God grows us when we're right in the thick of it. Those hard moments, sleepless nights, and selfless days are part of our life for God's divine purpose. "[Family life] is the sphere in which God is at work on us, shaping and molding us, that we may become people who genuinely share his life of love."[2]

Sure, when it comes to the spiritual disciplines, we have to be creative. And our spiritual growth practices will look a lot different than they did B.C. But the depth of our moment-by-moment encounter with God need not suffer because we're moms; in fact, it is *as moms* that our faith can flourish! It is *as a mom* that you will come to comprehend God's love in a life-changing way. It is *as a mom* that you discover the depth of God's grace and forgiveness as you forgive your own children. It is *as a mom* that you come face-to-face with your desperate need for God's presence and help.

For this is God's calling on your life—this is his purpose for you *right now*—this is the privilege he's entrusted to you. And it is in the real-life moments of motherhood that God will meet you and change you so that he can accomplish his good purpose in you and through you.

179

talk about it

Discuss these questions with a friend or a small group of other moms.

1. When you reflect on your current joys and struggles as a mom, how do you think God is using the sphere of family life to mold and shape you?

2. Look back at your spiritual-growth efforts over the past few years. Would you describe them more as "trying hard" or "training wisely"? What's the difference?

3. How has the training of practicing spiritual disciplines during your journey through this book affected your relationship with Christ? with others?

4. Which of the disciplines was most challenging for you? Why? What did God teach you through the challenge?

5. When it comes to the renovation God is doing in your heart and life, what next step are you thinking about taking?

try it: my training plan

Take some time to pray and reflect on all God has shown you as you've journeyed with him through the spiritual disciplines. When you're ready, use this template to identify some next steps you will take to "train yourself to be godly" (1 Tim. 4:7).

1. Which discipline do you sense God is prompting you to explore further?

2. How do you believe God wants you to change and grow through the practice of this discipline?

3. How long do you want to explore this discipline? (Though God may lead you to work on it longer than you think, it is helpful to identify a timeframe, for example, "I will focus on my spiritual training through the discipline of simplicity for the next four weeks.")

4. What are some specific actions or practices you plan to do? (For ideas, review the Putting It into Action and Try This suggestions in the various chapters or seek counsel from a pastor or mentor.)

181

action step or spiritual practice	when i'll do it	how often i'll do it	people or resources i'll need

If you want to keep this discussion going, join me in conversation about life, motherhood, and spiritual growth at www.kellitrujillo.com. I'd love to hear from you!

resources

There are lots of great resources available on all of the topics mentioned in this book. Here are a few that will get you started!

general resources on spiritual disciplines

Celebration of Discipline by Richard Foster (HarperSanFrancisco)

Devotional Classics, edited by Richard J. Foster and James Bryan Smith (HarperSanFrancisco)

Heart, Soul, and Money by Craig L. Blomberg (College Press)

Holiness for Ordinary People by Keith Drury (Wesleyan Publishing House)

The Life You've Always Wanted by John Ortberg (Zondervan)

Mudhouse Sabbath by Lauren F. Winner (Paraclete Press)

Practicing Our Faith, edited by Dorothy C. Bass (Jossey-Bass)

The Practice of the Presence of God with Spiritual Maxims by Brother Lawrence (Revell)

Receiving the Day by Dorothy C. Bass (Jossey-Bass)

Spiritual Disciplines Handbook by Adele Ahlberg Calhoun (InterVarsity Press)

Water My Soul: Cultivating the Interior Life by Luci Shaw (Zondervan)

Whole Prayer by Walter Wangerin Jr. (Zondervan)

With Unveiled Faces: Experience Intimacy with God through Spiritual Disciplines by Keith Drury (Wesleyan Publishing House)

bible study guides

Becoming a Woman of Excellence or *Intimacy With God* by Cynthia Heald (NavPress)

The Fruit of the Spirit Bible Studies series (Zondervan)

Lectio Divina Bible Studies (Wesleyan Publishing House)

LifeGuide Bible Study series (InterVarsity)

Precept Upon Precept Bible Study series by Kay Arthur (Precept Ministries)

Sisters in Faith Bible Studies (Wesleyan Publishing House)

The study features included in *The Renovaré Spiritual Formation Bible* (HarperSanFrancisco)

Spiritual Disciplines Bible Studies series by Janet L. Johnson (InterVarsity)

bible commentaries and study tools

Jesus and the Gospels by Craig L. Blomberg (Broadman and Holman)

New Bible Dictionary (InterVarsity Press)

The Pillar New Testament Commentary series (Eerdmans)

Wycliffe Bible Dictionary (Hendrickson Publishers)

Vine's Complete Expository Dictionary of Old and New Testament Words (Thomas Nelson)

Zondervan Illustrated Bible Backgrounds Commentary series (Zondervan)

Wesleyan Bible Commentary Series (Wesleyan Publishing House)

fair trade and living wage resources

www.equalexchange.com

www.globalcrafts.org

store.gxonlinestore.org

www.tenthousandvillages.com

www.transfairusa.org

notes

introduction

1. *Webster's New World College Dictionary*, 3rd ed. (Cleveland, Ohio: Macmillan, 1997).

chapter 2

Notes on Sidebars

Thomas à Kempis, "The Imitation of Christ" in *Spiritual Classics*, eds. Richard J. Foster and Emily Griffin (San Francisco: HarperSanFrancisco, 2000), 149.

Søren Kierkegaard, *Provocations*, ed. Charles E. Moore (Farmington, Pa.: The Plough, 1999), 371.

Notes on Chapter Text

1. Dallas Willard, *The Spirit of the Disciplines* (San Francisco: HarperSanFrancisco, 1988), 161.

2. Duke University Health System, "Give Your Family a Rest from Stress," Duke University, http://www.dukehealth.org/tips/tip_200311041 62120372 (accessed October 4, 2006).

3. Sleep expert Dr. Marc Weissbluth outlines what he considers to be healthy patterns of napping for young children, explaining that infants should average two or three lengthy naps per day while toddlers may nap only once or twice. A healthy pattern for two-, three-, and four-year-olds is to nap most days for one to three hours. Many five- and six-year-olds nap for one to two hours several times a week, while others have outgrown naps all together. (Marc Weissbluth, *Healthy Sleep Habits, Happy Child* (New York: Ballantine, 1999), 128–42, 182, 184, 207.)

4. "Facts and Figures about our TV Habit," TV Turnoff Network, http://www.tvturnoff.org/images/facts&figs/factsheets/FactsFigs.pdf (accessed October 4, 2006).

5. "Television and the Family," American Academy of Pediatrics, http://www.aap.org/family/tv1.htm (accessed October 4, 2006).

6. Ibid.

7. Katharina A. von Schlegel, "Be Still My Soul," *Hymns for the Family of God* (Nashville: Paragon, 1976), 77.

chapter 3

Note on Sidebar

Bruce Demarest, *Soul Guide* (Colorado Springs: NavPress, 2003), 94. Emphasis added.

Notes on Chapter Text

1. Forty-five percent of those surveyed by The Barna Group in 2005 reported that they read the Bible during a typical week. "The Bible" in *Barna by Topic*, The Barna Group, http://www.barna.org/flexpage.aspx?Page=Topic&TopicID=7 (accessed October 4, 2006).

2. Ignatius of Loyola, *The Spiritual Exercises of St. Ignatius of Loyola,* trans. Elder Mullan, S.J., (New York: P. J. Kenedy and Sons, 1914). Public domain. Available at *Christian Classics Ethereal Library*, Calvin College, http://www.ccel.org/ccel/ignatius/exercises.titlepage.html (accessed October 4, 2006).

chapter 4

Notes on Sidebars

Walter Wangerin Jr., *Whole Prayer* (Grand Rapids, Mich.: Zondervan, 1998), 206.

Adele Ahlberg Calhoun, *Spiritual Disciplines Handbook* (Downers Grove, Ill.: InterVarsity, 2005), 205.

Notes on Chapter Text

1. Janet L. Hopson, "Fetal Psychology" *Psychology Today*, September/October 1998, 44–50. Also Arlene Eisenberg, Heidi E. Murkoff, and Sandee E. Hathaway, *What to Expect When You're Expecting* (New York: Workman, 1996), 187, 215.

2. Thomas Merton, *New Seeds of Contemplation* (New York: New Directions Books, 1961), 217.

3. "The Keeping of Cell and Silence" (ch. 4) in *The Statues of the Carthusian Order*, The Carthusian Order, http://www.chartreux.org/en/frame.html (accessed October 4, 2006).

4. C. S. Lewis, "The Efficacy of Prayer" in *The World's Last Night and Other Essays* (San Diego, Calif.: Harcourt, 1987), 8.

5. Brother Lawrence, "Second Letter" in *The Practice of the Presence of God*, trans. Nicholas Herman (London: The Epworth Press, n.d.). Public domain. Christian Classics Ethereal Library at Calvin College, http://www.ccel.org/ccel/lawrence/practice.iv.ii.html (accessed October 4, 2006).

6. Brother Lawrence, "Fourth Conversation" in *The Practice of the Presence of God*, trans. Nicholas Herman (London: The Epworth Press, n.d.). Public domain. Christian Classics Ethereal Library at Calvin College, http://www.ccel.org/ccel/lawrence/practice.iii.iv.html (accessed October 4, 2006).

7. Brother Lawrence, "Maxims" in *The Practice of the Presence of God* (Springdale, Pa.: Whitaker House, 1982), 70; emphasis added.

8. Lewis, 8.

chapter 5

Notes on Sidebars

Dallas Willard, *The Divine Conspiracy* (San Francisco: HarperSanFrancisco, 1998), 16.

A. W. Tozer, *The Pursuit of God* (Camp Hill, Pa.: Christian Publications, 1993), 113.

Luci Shaw, *Water My Soul* (Grand Rapids, Mich.: Zondervan, 1998), 120.

Notes on Chapter Text

1. Walter Isaacson, *Benjamin Franklin—An American Life* (New York: Simon and Schuster, 2003), 89–90.

2. Keith Drury, *With Unveiled Faces* (Indianapolis: Wesleyan, 2005), 96.

3. Andrew Murray, *Humility* (Fort Washington, Pa.: Christian Literature Crusade, 1995), 117–18.

chapter 6

Notes on Sidebars

Oswald Chambers, *My Utmost for His Highest* (Grand Rapids, Mich.: Discovery House, 1994), February 25.

Mother Teresa, *A Simple Path,* ed. Lucinda Vardley (New York: Ballantine, 1995), 79.

Notes on Chapter Text

1. Mother Teresa, *Simple Path,* 114.

2. Eugene H. Peterson, *A Long Obedience in the Same Direction,* 2nd ed. (Downers Grove, Ill.: InterVarsity, 2000), 66.

3. Mother Teresa, *Simple Path,* 137.

4. Ibid., 115.

chapter 7

Notes on Sidebars

"Evangelism" in *Barna by Topic,* The Barna Group, http://www.barna.org/flexpage.aspx?page=Topic&TopicID=18 (accessed October 4, 2006).

Ana Maria Piñeda, "Hospitality," in *Practicing Our Faith,* ed. Dorothy C. Bass (San Francisco: Jossey-Bass, 1997), 32.

Notes on Chapter Text

1. Rick Richardson, *Evangelism Outside the Box* (Downers Grove, Ill.: InterVarsity, 2000), 93.

2. Richardson, *Outside the Box,* 95.

3. Jane Jarrell, "Hospitality—A Spa for the Soul," *MOMSense,* March/April 2006, 24.

chapter 8

Notes on Sidebars

Richard Foster, *Freedom of Simplicity* (New York: HarperCollins, 1981), 62.

Craig L. Blomberg, *Heart, Soul, and Money* (Joplin, Mo.: College Press, 2000), 56.

John Wesley, *A Longing for Holiness,* ed. Keith Beasley-Topliffe (Nashville: Upper Room, 1997), 16.

Blomberg, *Heart, Soul,* 56.

Notes on Chapter Text

1. John Zmirak, "The Simple Life Redux: An Interview with Eric Brende," God Spy, http://www.godspy.com/reviews/The-Simple-Life-

Redux-An-Interview-with-Eric-Brende-by-John-Zmirak.cfm (accessed October 4, 2006).

2. Eric Brende, "No Technology? No Problem" in *What Matters*., MIT Alumni Association, http://alum.mit.edu/ne/whatmatters/200410/index. html (accessed October 4, 2006).

3. John Rosemond, *Because I Said So!* (Kansas City, Mo.: Andrews McMeel, 1996), 207.

4. Marianne McGinnis, "Set-Free," *Prevention*, http://www.prevention.com/article/0,,s1-6-79-136-6799-1,00.html (accessed October 4, 2006).

5. "New Study Finds Children Age Zero to Six Spend As Much Time With TV, Computers and Video Games as Playing Outside," The Henry J. Kaiser Family Foundation, http://www.kff.org/entmedia/entmedia102803nr.cfm (accessed October 4, 2006).

6. Rosemond, *Because I Said So!*, 74.

7. "Money 101: Top Things to Know," CNNMoney.com, http://money.cnn.com/pf/101/lessons/9/ (accessed October 4, 2006).

8. William T. Cavanaugh, "When Enough is Enough," *Sojourners*, May 2005, http://www.sojo.net/index.cfm?action=magazine.article&issue=soj0505&article=050510 (accessed October 4, 2006).

9. Augustine, *Confessions*, trans. John K. Ryan (Garden City, N.Y.: Doubleday, 1960), 44.

10. Foster, *Simplicity*, 62.

11. R. Paul Stevens, "Stewardship" in *The Complete Book of Everyday Christianity*, eds. Robert Banks and R. Paul Stevens (Downer's Grove, Ill.: InterVarsity, 1997), 962.

12. "Hunger Facts: International," Bread for the World, www.bread.org/learn/hunger-basics/hunger-facts-international.html (accessed October 4, 2006).

13. Foster, *Simplicity*, 3

14. Isaac Watts, "When I Survey the Wondrous Cross," in *Hymns for the Family of God* (Nashville: Paragon, 1976), 258. Public Domain.

chapter 9

Notes on Sidebars

Richard Foster, *Celebration of Discipline*, 20th anniversary ed. (San Francisco: HarperSanFrancisco, 1998), 55.

M. Shawn Copeland, "Saying Yes and Saying No" in *Practicing our Faith*, ed. Dorothy C. Bass (San Francisco: Jossey-Bass, 1997), 60.

Notes on Chapter Text

1. Keith Drury, *With Unveiled Faces: Experience Intimacy with God through Spiritual Disciplines* (Indianapolis: Wesleyan, 2005), 13–14.

2. John Wesley, "Sermon on the Mount (VII)—Sermon 27," public domain. http://gbgm-umc.org/umw/wesley/serm-027.stm (accessed October 4, 2006).

3. Dietrich Bonhoeffer, *The Cost of Discipleship* (New York: Simon and Schuster, 1995), 169.

4. Calhoun, *Spiritual Disciplines Handbook* (Downers Grove, Ill.: InterVarsity, 2005), 220.

5. Lauren F. Winner, *Girl Meets God* (New York: Random House, 2002), 128–29.

6. Dietrich Bonhoeffer, *The Cost of Discipleship* (New York: Simon and Schuster, 1995), 44.

7. Anna Marlis Burgard, ed., *Hallelujah—The Poetry of Classic Hymns* (Berkeley, Calif.: Celestial Arts, 2005), 83.

chapter 10

Notes on Sidebars

Eugene H. Peterson, *A Long Obedience in the Same Direction*, 2nd ed. (Downers Grove, Ill.: Intervarsity, 2000), 175.

Dietrich Bonhoeffer, *Life Together*, trans. John W. Doberstein (San Francisco: HarperSanFrancisco, 1954), 23.

Bruce Demarest, *Satisfy Your Soul* (Colorado Springs: NavPress, 1999), 199.

Notes on Chapter Text

1. Bonhoeffer, *Life Together*, 112.

2. William A. Barry and William J. Connolly, *The Practice of Spiritual Direction* (San Francisco: HarperSanFrancisco, 1986), 8.

3. Barry and Connolly, *Spiritual Direction*, 6–7. Emphasis added.

4. Bonhoeffer, *Life Together*, 21.

chapter 11

Notes on Sidebars

Charles H. Spurgeon, *The Treasury of David*, ed. David O. Fuller (Grand Rapids, Mich.: Kregel, 1976), 404.

Marva J. Dawn, *Reaching Out without Dumbing Down* (Grand Rapids, Mich.: Eerdmans, 1995), 57–58.

Notes on Chapter Text

1. Donald S. Whitney, *Spiritual Disciplines for the Christian Life* (Colorado Springs: NavPress, 1991), 88–89.

2. Dallas Willard, *The Spirit of the Disciplines* (San Francisco: HarperSanFrancisco, 1988), 179.

3. Richard Foster, *Celebration of Discipline*, 20th anniversary ed. (San Francisco: HarperSanFrancisco, 1998), 191, 195.

4. John Ortberg, *The Life You've Always Wanted* (Grand Rapids, Mich.: Zondervan, 2002), 67.

5. Dorothy C. Bass, *Receiving the Day* (San Francisco: Jossey-Bass, 2000), 62.

6. Harold M. Best, *Unceasing Worship* (Downers Grove, Ill.: InterVarsity, 2003), 40.

chapter 12

1. John Ortberg, *The Life You've Always Wanted* (Grand Rapids, Mich.: Zondervan, 2002), 43. Emphasis mine.

2. Gilbert Meilaender, *Things That Count* (Wilmington, Del.: ISI Books, 2000), 97.

For more on motherhood and spiritual disciplines, visit www.kellitrujillo.com.